Old Parish

About the Author

Ciarán Murphy is a podcaster with Second Captains and a GAA columnist with the *Irish Times*. His first book, *This is the Life: Days and Nights in the GAA*, was shortlisted for Eason Sports Book of the Year at the Irish Book Awards.

To Dermot,

Old Parish

Ciarán Murphy

thanks so much for the chat — I loved it

UP OUR SIDE !!

SANDYCOVE

an imprint of

PENGUIN BOOKS

SANDYCOVE

UK | USA | Canada | Ireland | Australia
India | New Zealand | South Africa

Sandycove is part of the Penguin Random House group of companies
whose addresses can be found at global.penguinrandomhouse.com

Penguin Random House UK,
One Embassy Gardens, 8 Viaduct Gardens, London SW11 7BW

penguin.co.uk

First published 2025
001

Copyright © Ciarán Murphy, 2025

The moral right of the author has been asserted

The poem 'All-Ireland Final' by Theo Dorgan on p. 179 is from *Nine Bright Shiners*
(Dedalus Press, Dublin 2014) and reproduced with permission.

Penguin Random House values and supports copyright.
Copyright fuels creativity, encourages diverse voices, promotes freedom
of expression and supports a vibrant culture. Thank you for purchasing
an authorized edition of this book and for respecting intellectual property
laws by not reproducing, scanning or distributing any part of it by any
means without permission. You are supporting authors and enabling
Penguin Random House to continue to publish books for everyone.
No part of this book may be used or reproduced in any manner for the
purpose of training artificial intelligence technologies or systems. In accordance
with Article 4(3) of the DSM Directive 2019/790, Penguin Random House
expressly reserves this work from the text and data mining exception.

Set in 15/18 pt Perpetua MT Pro
Typeset by Falcon Oast Graphic Art Ltd
Printed and bound in Great Britain by Clays Ltd, Elcograf S.p.A.

The authorized representative in the EEA is Penguin Random House Ireland,
Morrison Chambers, 32 Nassau Street, Dublin D02 YH68

A CIP catalogue record for this book is available from the British Library

ISBN: 978–1–844–88689–0

Do mo shinsir

1

I have a distinct memory of playing hurling as a kid on my local GAA pitch in Milltown, in north-east Galway. I must have been injured or incapacitated in some way at the time, because I recall pucking around with my dad in the middle of the pitch while my Gaelic football teammates ran a couple of laps around us.

I would have been no more than eleven or twelve, and I remember getting an awful slagging. I've asked the fella most likely to have done the slagging about that day. He broadly confirmed my memory of the event, and said something that chimed very precisely with my impression at the time: 'No one else from Milltown had a hurl, so I'd say you did get a bit of abuse!'

In one sense, there is nothing surprising about this little incident: any deviation from the norm when you were a kid back then meant you copped a bit of flak. And north-east Galway really wasn't hurling country: that doesn't begin until you get close to the Dublin–Galway railway line.

But the more I've thought about it, the wilder it seems. My father and I were playing one of the two major GAA field sports, on a GAA pitch, in a county that might well have played in the All-Ireland hurling final that year (if the year in question was 1993, when I was eleven), and this was nevertheless deemed to be some kind of subversive act. I certainly didn't do it again down at the pitch in Milltown, though it was not particularly uncommon for my dad and me to puck around a bit in our backyard during my childhood. Dad had played hurling as a youngfella in Waterford, and we had a couple of hurleys in our shed.

For most of the young people in our village, it was different. If both your parents grew up in or around north Galway or south Mayo, your exposure to hurling was fleeting at best. For most, it was non-existent. I grew up supporting the successful Galway hurling team of the late 1980s, watching every bit of hurling on television that I could. But if you lived in that part of Ireland – as in so many other parts of Ireland – your interaction with the game was always as a spectator, never as a participant. To actually pick up a hurley was a waste of time. It might even have been looked upon as an affectation.

Two books about the history of hurling were published in the 1970s. The first was called *Camán: 2000 Years of Hurling in Ireland*. The title of the second – *Iomáint in*

Éirinn Anallód sé sin ó Thosach Ama, Go Bliain 1884 — could have been read as a rebuke to the first. Why read a book that contains a mere 2,000 years of history when you could read one that traces the story of hurling back to 'the beginning of time'?

There are two Irelands. In the one I grew up in, hurling was not the done thing. In the other Ireland, it is very much the done thing — and no one there will ever be allowed to sell hurling short. It is quite convenient for its many hagiographers and obsessives that, when they say it is the most beautiful sport in the world to watch — 'the greatest game that was ever played by any man', as Anthony Daly called it at the end of the 2018 All-Ireland final — the bombast is probably justified.

Hurling has elements that make it almost cartoonishly mythic. Take, for example, Joe Canning — by general acclamation one of the five best hurlers of all time. Canning comes from the part of Galway where hurling is the done thing. He played in his first senior All-Ireland final in 2012, and the hurley he played with that day was a hurley he made himself.

It's like something from a fable — the warrior sharpening his own blade, forging his own sword, in the days before the battle. Canning scored a goal ten minutes into that final that was so good, so thrilling to watch, it seemed likely to bring Croke Park crashing down upon itself. He must have felt like the king of the world in that moment... and then again forty-five seconds later, when he imperiously blocked down a Kilkenny clearance, somehow magicked the ball into his hand, and whipped it back over the bar for a sumptuous point.

Imagine the adrenalin flowing through him at that moment — you can picture it travelling all the way out to the bas of this hurley of his own creation.

And then, with fifteen minutes to go, the hurley was broken irreparably and Canning had to hit a free to force a replay with the last puck of the game, using another hurley altogether. If the hurley that broke really was imbued with magical powers, then Canning was able to corral its replacement into finding the target and forcing the replay.

It's not just Canning who seems connected to some deep mythic energy. Tipperary's Ronan Maher regularly finds himself hip-to-hip with Limerick's Aaron Gillane, another of the game's deadliest shooters, who uses a hurley Maher himself made. These people are guardians of the game in the truest possible sense.

Or what about Maher's fellow Tipperary man, Brendan Cummins, who throughout his career as one of the greatest goalkeepers of all time made sure year after year to take part in the Poc Fada. This is a competition held in the Cooley mountains in Louth every year, where hurlers compete to traverse a course five kilometres in length in the smallest number of pucks.

The course follows the journey that Setanta, the boy who would become Cúchulainn, took from his home at Dún Dealgan to King Conchubar's court at Emain Macha, hitting his sliotar out in front of him for the duration of the journey.

This is a fable from over two thousand years ago – and the competition based on it draws some of the biggest names in the game every year. Cummins won the Poc Fada nine times, but he wasn't the only big name in senior inter-county hurling to compete. Ger Cunningham of Cork, the best goalie of the 1980s, won it seven times. A contemporary of Cummins, Davy Fitzgerald of Clare, won it twice. Pat Hartigan and Tommy Quaid, two more well-known players from Limerick, were winners as well.

But hurling's unique mystique is not merely a function of its ancientness, its place in Irish myth, or the way its racy-of-the-soil heroes craft their own weapons. It is also a function of the game itself, because at its best modern hurling is quite simply a stunning thing to behold. It requires outrageous hand–eye coordination, which must be executed under conditions unique among the great ball-striking games: while running at full speed, and with someone attempting to tackle you.

As an example of what hurling is like at its best, we might go to the forty-sixth minute of the Cork vs Limerick All-Ireland semi-final of 2024. Limerick's Cian

Lynch hand-passes the ball to Tom Morrissey, only for him to be set upon by Declan Dalton and Shane Barrett of Cork. They force him to cough up possession, but he somehow manages to regather the ball and hand-pass to Cian Lynch. Tim O'Mahony grabs Lynch, monsters him out of the way, and regains the sliotar for Cork. Shane Barrett gets a hand-pass from him, and through a cluster of bodies he sets Brian Hayes away. Hayes plays a one-two with Niall O'Leary, but a flick past Mike Casey only results in giving the ball to Dan Morrissey. He hand-passes the ball to Declan Hannon who is running a support line, and Seamus Flanagan, the Limerick full-forward, takes it from him. He delivers a seventy-five-metre pass in towards Aaron Gillane, who beats Ciaran Joyce in the air with his hurley and knocks the ball down to himself. He gets the ball into his hand quick as a flash, then under-arms an unorthodox stick-pass to Gearóid Hegarty, who sizes up his man and hits a bullet of a shot at goal. Patrick Collins makes a stunning save, but the rebound comes out towards Gillane. He scuffs his shot, and is swallowed up by three Cork defenders. Robert Downey comes out of defence, finds Declan Dalton inside his own 65, and he points down the other end. It's fifty-two seconds from Dalton's tackle on Tom Morrissey to Dalton's point – and that passage of play included seven turnovers, two goal chances, and then a point at the opposite end, all done at an exceptionally high level of skill and intensity.

I remember listening to this game in my car, and the sound emanating from my radio at that moment was nothing short of mass hysteria. It was as if the entire capacity crowd in Croke Park had lost all control of their emotions. I watched the game back two hours later and experienced the same feelings myself, even knowing the final result. It was glorious chaos. You can make all the arguments in the world for any other sport, but I just can't see how it matches up. Hurling is absolutely in a world of its own when it is played like that.

And yet ... there was laughter from my peers when I played it on our GAA pitch.

This book is, in part, an exploration of a big, and very old, story: the story of hurling's place in Irish life. It also tells a much smaller story, one from my own life across a few months in 2024. As of the start of that year, I had never felt the dull thud of a sliotar into my hand in a competitive game. I had never received a whack of a hurley across my thighs or my arms. I had never had my fingers softened up by a wild pull in the air as I went up to catch a ball.

And it seemed to me that if I never experienced those things, I would never be able to gain a deep sense of the culture of the sport, the essence of it. I felt that in my bones, and it bothered me.

I had a few questions I wanted to answer. Why did I feel like less of an Irishman for not having played hurling?

Why wasn't I given the chance to play it competitively as a kid? And: if I were to take it up now, at forty-one years of age, how bad could I possibly be?

2

There was one hurley in our utility room in Milltown that I remember with particular vividness from childhood. About 10 per cent of the bas was missing and the name 'S. Frampton' was written down the side of it. The S. Frampton in question was Stephen Frampton, who played inter-county hurling for Waterford – my father's native county, as I've mentioned – for eleven years.

Frampton's career ended after he walked out of the panel at the start of 2002. Unfortunately for him, that was the year Waterford bridged a thirty-nine-year gap between Munster championship wins. Precisely how his hurley ended up in our utility room is a mystery, but it must have had something to do with my uncle Deaglán, who was a teacher in De La Salle College, where Frampton went to school, and who was involved in the De La Salle club in the city, rivals of Frampton's club Ballygunner.

Perhaps some De La Salle man had chopped down on Frampton one summer's evening in Waterford city.

Perhaps, as Frampton reacted to the assault, he threw his hurley to the sideline, only for it to be picked up by my cousin Raymond or Paddy maybe, and the hurley then passed from their house, to our house, to my hand.

If Frampton's hurley, at the moment of its creation, dreamed of making the ultimate sacrifice for Waterford hurling – maybe getting smashed in two as its owner made a frantic last-minute dive to hook a Kilkenny forward about to hit the winning goal in an All-Ireland final – then spending the autumn of its years lightly used in a football-mad house in north-east Galway would have seemed like a strange kind of purgatory.

The hurley in question was safe from the threat of instant destruction in our house. The fact that we not only tolerated a hurley with a portion of its bas missing, but kept it around for an entire generation, would suggest as much. We didn't ask much of the hurleys in our backyard, obviously.

I was the youngest of four boys, and as my brothers moved out of the house I got more used to the idea of hitting a tennis ball off the gable end, either with a tennis racquet for the two weeks of Wimbledon, or with a hurley. But the vast majority of my free time was spent practising my Gaelic football skills off the side of our house.

I went off to college, and started work in Dublin. For years, I didn't pick up a hurley at all. I saw plenty of hurling in Croke Park in that time – including, in 2005, all four quarter-finals, both semi-finals and the final, which Galway lost to Cork. As Galway's stock dipped, Waterford's continued to rise. I was devastated to see Waterford lose to Limerick in the 2007 All-Ireland semi-final, a game they really should have won. I sat beside my uncle Deaglán for Waterford's first All-Ireland final appearance in forty-five years in 2008 . . . and saw them lose by twenty-three points to Kilkenny.

Around that time, my friend group moved out towards Stoneybatter. If we were congregating in the Phoenix Park on a summer's day, a call would inevitably go out to bring whatever sports equipment you had in your house with you, just to be messing around with. Most of the time that was an O'Neills Gaelic football or a soccer ball. Sometimes that would be an American football, or a rugby ball. And at some stage in that part of our lives, hurleys entered the rotation.

Hurling was more fun in this setup than almost any other sport precisely because it was difficult. Kicking a Gaelic football to each other got boring in a hurry, and so too did games of one-touch or two-touch soccer. Trying to kick drop-goals is a laugh, but one rugby ball between three lads, or more, meant you had to wait your turn. But there was satisfaction in going for a puck-around because we were all awful enough to get a sense of achievement in just being able to fulfil the most basic of 'hit-ball-catch-ball' functions. We were not aware of following in the footsteps of Michael Cusack, whose early outings with the new Dublin Hurling Club in the Phoenix Park in early 1884 were a precursor to the founding of the GAA later that year. And we were not entirely sure of what we were doing with a hurley in our hands. But it was enjoyable.

I had never played a game of hurling in my life. I was an unreliable striker of the ball, prone to the odd fresh-air shot, and magnificently unskilled. I was also, by a distance, the best hurler in the group. Mark Horgan was a Gaelic footballer who hadn't played Gaelic football in years. Collie McKeown was a soccer player who had played neither Gaelic football nor hurling in his life. But there was something in the challenge of hurling that continued to attract us all to the idea of a puck-around. One of us would move house, a hurley might get lost, and we'd go to the middle aisle in Lidl – or, if we were feeling particularly flaithiúlach, to a sports shop in town – to replace it.

I mustn't overstate this. We might have pucked around twice or three times a year in the summertime. As Covid lingered, the regularity of our meetings went up a notch or two: it was an excuse to get out of the house and have a few cans of beer together. I found I had gotten to the stage where fresh-air shots were becoming a thing of the past, at least until we'd started our third drink.

Once I was reasonably sure of hitting the ball every time I threw it up, I grew more confident. I could find either of my friends from twenty or thirty metres away, and their good-natured curses as they failed to catch the ball, or to control it on their hurl, gave me a smug sense of superiority. This was one area of our friendship where I towered above them. And it felt good.

As Christmas 2022 approached, and my brothers and I discussed what we wanted as a gift, I asked my brother Paul for a hurley and a few sliotars. He's heavily involved with St Mary's GAA club in Athenry, where he's been living since 2005, and I knew he'd have a source at least slightly better than the middle aisle of a German-owned supermarket.

That Christmas hurley saw more action than any other hurley I'd ever had. This was in no small part due to the slow-dawning realization on the part of my daft dog Pickles that if she just drops the ball I'm hitting for her (rather than running around with it in her mouth for minutes on end), I'll hit it for her again, and she can chase after it again. This canine cognitive breakthrough alone meant I hit a lot of balls in 2023.

There's a GAA pitch right beside my home in Dublin 8. If you spend even twenty minutes on a pitch with a hurley and a couple of sliotars, it would take unbelievable discipline not to hit at least ten shots at a goalpost . . . and I do not have unbelievable discipline.

My friends became ever more unreliable as fatherhood impinged on their free time. My hurling life was now quite literally one man and his dog. But I loved the feeling of getting to a place where I was reasonably sure that every time I swung, I was going to make contact with the ball. This was an exceptionally low bar, but one I was still happy to clear. You could practise hitting off your left side, your right side – the dog didn't care.

These twenty- or thirty-minute interludes with Pickles became the highlight of my day. I'd walk out towards the 45-metre line, set my feet and swing at goal. I'd stand out near the sideline, imagine I was Joe Canning and arrow a shot off towards the far post, begging it to draw slowly back in towards the goal. I'd move closer to the end-line, shorten the grip on the hurley and try to hit a score from an acute angle.

At some stage, maybe anyone would feel compelled to see if hitting balls over the bar from forty metres out, uncontested and from a standing position, with no non-Labradoodle witnesses, was a skill transferable to the chaos and calamity of an actual hurling game. Or maybe I was the only middle-aged madman who entertained such thoughts.

It almost made things worse that I had actually played thirty minutes of hurling – in Croke Park of all places.

A group of GAA journalists used to play the employees of Croke Park in an annual charity Gaelic football game in the Big House. One year some bright spark had the idea that we should play one half of hurling and one half of football. I rocked up with no hurley, no helmet, and no clue what I was doing. I was lining out at centre-forward for the football team, so that's where I was put for the hurlers as well. What struck me immediately was how alien the whole thing felt from the moment the sliotar was thrown in. Having been hastily provided with the tools of the trade, I could barely fasten my helmet. I had no idea where to go on the pitch. I had no idea how far I could hit the ball, and I had no idea how to move the ball on if I got it.

Having run to wherever the ball was not for the first twenty minutes, I somehow managed to inveigle a shooting chance from about forty-five metres out, into the Davin Stand end, in the final minutes of the half. It is indicative of just how pedestrian was the pace of this game that I was gloriously unhurried while taking the shot. It went inches wide on the Cusack Stand side. And that was that.

I was working for *Off the Ball* on Newstalk at the time, listening to Jamesie O'Connor and Daithí Regan break down games in granular detail. They'd speak of catching the ball with your 'wrong hand', or describe a player who had 'a cack-handed grip'. This jargon was pleasingly unfamiliar – it made me curious to know more. But what could you really know if you've never played the game?

Ger Loughnane is on record as saying that if you haven't started hurling by the age of seven, it's probably too late.

So at the start of 2024, looking ahead to my forty-second birthday in July of that year, I knew I was behind schedule.

But what if I just went for it? What if I decided to join my father's old club in Waterford, An Sean Phobal (aka Old Parish), moved down from Dublin for six months, and sought ground-floor entry to the world of the Hurling Man?

Spending six months in Waterford would require some arranging. Work was the easiest thing to sort out. We had gotten pretty used to broadcasting our daily Second Captains podcasts remotely during Covid, and if I could spend a day or two a week in Dublin, the other five or six wouldn't present any major difficulty.

Accommodation was also manageable. I'd live with my uncle John to begin with, and then my wife, Gill, would come down and join me once her teaching year had finished.

The GAA transfer was more complex. My football club in Dublin, Templeogue Synge Street, was happy to facilitate me. But there was the Waterford County Board to deal with, and of course I'd have to make sure that Old Parish themselves would be OK with my joining up with them for a summer. My family history with the club dates back to my grandfather's time, in the 1930s, but it's not exactly easy to walk into a dressing room full of lads you've never met before, tell them that you will be absolutely no use to them whatsoever, and expect them to be enthusiastically on board with whatever stunt it is that you're trying to pull.

On the other hand, An Sean Phobal is a tiny club, by any metric. Crucially, for me, it is also a dual-code club. They have only one team in each code, and there was by all accounts nearly complete crossover between the two playing panels. In 2024 they would be competing in the Junior B hurling championship in Waterford, having won the Junior C hurling championship the previous autumn. Their football team was in the Junior A championship. I had little to offer the hurling team, but I had played football my entire life, had managed to stay reasonably fit while doing it with Templeogue Synge Street for the previous seven years, and so might conceivably have something still to give on that front.

I told a friend about this rather strange plan of mine. Instead of focusing on the odd logistics, or the imminent danger that taking up hurling must present to a man of my age, Clare simply said, 'You know, I think it's admirable that you're willing to be this terrible at something when you're in your forties.' Far too many of us leave our experimentation behind us after our twenties.

It's the reason I never played a computer game in my life. And as the years advance, I get more and more set in my ways. You will not see me on a zipline. I will not be jumping out of planes. Triathlons hold no appeal to me. If the primary purpose of this project was for me to feel like a fish out of water in a sporting context, I could have joined a rugby club, or a cricket club. I might well have enjoyed myself immensely and come away with a brand-new understanding of a subset of society I'd never come into much contact with. But that wasn't really what I was after.

So what the hell was I doing this for? I think that what entranced me most about the idea of taking up hurling was that hurling people were GAA people: they were *my* people. I knew them in my bones. And yet I didn't know, intimately know, the game that brought them so much joy — and which caused them to look down upon Gaelic football, a sport I loved, with such disdain.

In January 2024 I stood in the Hugh Lane Gallery in Dublin with my brother Paul. We'd gone in to see an Andy Warhol exhibition, and now we were looking at 'The Tipperary Hurler', by Seán Keating. The hurler of the title has his hurley gripped tightly with both hands. Every muscle in both his forearms bulges, the veins protrude. His face is set in a grim, determined expression. A rural idyll spreads out behind his back. He is ready for whatever the day brings. It is a visual representation of the sort of thing W. B. Yeats was talking about in that poem we all did in secondary school, 'The Fisherman'. We are meant to look at him and think, *Yes, this is what an Irishman is supposed to look like. Behold this descendant of Cúchulainn, this wise and simple man.*

I knew in my heart that not playing hurling didn't make

me any less of an Irishman – not really. But I also felt there was something about the Irish spirit that I wouldn't have access to if I never tried it.

I could, of course, have just joined a hurling club in Dublin. St Kevin's hurling club play their home games at the Templeogue Synge Street home grounds. Many of the Templeogue Synge Street youngsters play their hurling or camogie with Faugh's, a storied club based just down the road. There was no shortage of options in Dublin. But I was eager for more than just the game. I wanted an immersive experience. I wanted to get out of the city. I wanted to feel like a real fish out of water, not just a tourist. And yes – I wanted to do it for my dad.

He hadn't played for the club for fifty years. I remember going to an Old Parish football game with him in Cappoquin when I couldn't have been any more than five or six and realizing, maybe for the first time, that this was Dad's real club, no matter how much effort he put into our club in Milltown.

That was always there, floating around in my head. There was also a visit I had made to Old Parish, after I'd been in Cork at a book signing the previous November. I had asked my aunt Joan if I could call in to see her in An Rinn on the way back to Dublin. She told me that she'd be at a coffee morning in the Halla Colmán beside the church in An Sean Phobal at around the time I'd be passing through, and that I should call in.

I'd barely had time to tell her that would be fine before a message appeared in the Old Parish GAA club WhatsApp group (of which my father is a member), saying that 'prominent author' Ciarán Murphy would be signing copies of his book in the village that Saturday between 1 and 2 p.m. A number of my cousins came down to say hello, including Michael and Tom Hogan, my father's first cousins, who both still lived in Old Parish and were involved with the club. In truth, that was the day the idea first really caught my imagination. Maybe this could be done?

When I told Dad my plan, I was eager to know that he wasn't going to be stressed out by it – concerned that I might not be accepted, or just worried in the non-specific way that parents seem to get about their kids as they get older. His reaction was just what I wanted it to be: Go for it, you lunatic. But be sure and ring your uncle John first. He should be the first to know.

Uncle John is different from his siblings. Dad was a County Council official for his entire professional life, Deaglán an Irish and maths teacher in De La Salle College in Waterford city. Joan got married to Tom de Faoite just down the road in An Rinn, and was a *bean an tí* for decades with the Irish college there. Tony, Deaglán and Joan are not sombre people, but they have an outlook on life that would value propriety, seriousness, a certain way of doing things.

John is . . . less concerned about such matters. He is a storyteller, a raconteur, a businessman, a horse-trader, a farmer, and a character of the first order. And as a result, his siblings love him beyond measure. My father can't mention his name without laughing. Other kinds of uncle might have been concerned about my fitting in, but John felt absolutely convinced that it would be fine once everyone found out that I was his nephew. I was, after all, a Murphy.

'So, John, I'm thinking of coming down to play hurling with An Sean Phobal. I'll probably have to live with you for a little while. And I'm going to write a book while I'm down there. Does that sound alright with you?'

A pause on the line, before 'OK so!' – said in the declarative tone of voice that I would come to enjoy listening to so much over the next six months. 'And will you play the football as well?' he asked me. I was pretty sure he was thinking of me as the footballer he might have seen playing for Milltown twenty years earlier. I decided that if I was going to play the poor mouth with regard to the hurling, there was no harm in telling him I was coming down to show the locals how to play the big ball. He appreciated the bombast, and then put me in touch with the club chairman, Michael Hogan, his first cousin – my first cousin once removed. And just like that, the wheels were in motion.

While I was mulling over the last few details, I had one

last intermediate football league game with Templeogue Synge Street, away to Clondalkin on a Sunday morning in mid-March. At one stage late in the first half, I went up to field a kick, caught the ball, called a mark, and then had a young lad thunder into my lower back with his knee while I was on the ground.

This . . . angered me. I got up and grabbed the lad by his collar. This led to a number of other Clondalkin lads getting involved, which led to a number of Synger lads getting involved, and I found myself in the middle of a kerfuffle. It quickly descended into farce when another Clondalkin player came in, grabbed me by the back of my collar, and ripped the jersey clean off my back, from collar to waistband.

Luckily I had some under-armour on underneath my jersey, so my ample man-boobs were kept out of sight of the general public. But it meant that when I was presented with the number 14 jersey from my last game for Synger for the foreseeable future as a permanent keepsake, it came in two parts.

That game safely negotiated, I went onto the GAA website and discovered that club transfers are now initiated online. There were six steps involved. First, An Sean Phobal would have to agree, then the GAA centrally would allow the transfer process to begin. Then Templeogue Synge Street would have to agree, then the Dublin County Board, then the Waterford County Board, and then the

GAA would rubber-stamp it. The first four steps happened inside forty-eight hours, and then I was made to wait for a few days. If Waterford County Board had wanted to make things difficult for me, they could well have done so. As it turned out, it was merely a processing delay. In the end, the whole thing took just over a week.

It had gone from an idle thought in my head, to a possibility, to a done deal in the space of a few weeks. I was an Old Parish clubman.

3

Mam was suitably amused by the latest twist in my peripatetic GAA career. 'Well, the best of luck with it,' she said. 'If you're writing about it all, I suppose you'll want to know about Milltown's hurling club, then.'

'Yeah, that was a bit of a pub-team thing though, wasn't it? It wasn't an actual . . . club? Right?'

'Milltown had a hurling club. In the 1950s. There was war over a dance in Tuam that was supposed to be a fundraiser for the hurling club. Sure Jim wrote an article in the *Tuam Herald* about it a few years ago.'

Of course, my uncle Jim Carney had the full story. I found the article, which described the club's first game, a challenge match against another new hurling club in the area, Seán Higgins's, in March 1956:

> The more experienced Seán Higgins', with JJ Hughes scoring four goals, won by two points, 4–3 to 4–1. Milltown's best were Walsh, Kelly, Murray, O'Hara and Heaney.

Pat Heaney was a legendary hurling man from Belmont, in the shadow of Culkin's Hill. He was a lean, wiry, very fit man who cycled everywhere. He fought the cause of the Clash of the Ash all his life, including turbulent encounters with Galway County Board and the Connacht Council. His indomitable spirit extended to supporting Galway hurling teams and as recently as the mid-1980s he cycled to Croke Park for an All-Ireland final. A Milltown mini-bus, driven by Tony Murphy, caught up with Pat on his bike on the bog road between Mountbellew and Ballyforan early on the Sunday morning but he cheerfully waved them on with his maroon and white flag.

This Pat Heaney character – how had I never heard of him? Tony Murphy, the driver of the Milltown minibus, was my own father. I read on:

The new Milltown club, named Michael Davitts, went on to play in North Board B grade competitions throughout the 1950s and I have a memory of watching a large group of men playing hurling at the local GAA Club pitch several times in the early 1960s. I was born and reared in the parish and in my teenage years I became aware that hurling had been played in the long shadow of football, which was considered by some club officials to be much more important!

For example, when the hurlers organized a fund-raising dance for the local CYMS Hall on a Sunday night in April 1956 it was advertised in the Tuam Herald as:

GAA Dance in Milltown. Music by
The Sylvians from Limerick.

Dancing 8.00 to 12 midnight. Admission 4 shillings.

A few weeks later the Herald carried a small advertisement stating that 'Milltown GAA Club wish to make it clear they had no connection with a dance advertised as a GAA dance.' It was signed by the GAA Club secretary.

The placing of this second ad suggested that the relationship between the two games in our tiny parish may have gotten off on the wrong foot. The football club could perhaps be forgiven for reacting when they saw what they thought was an attempt by the hurling club to raise funds under a false pretence. If a casual reader saw the advertisement for a GAA fundraising dance for Milltown, they would naturally have presumed it was for the football club. Even in a place as small as Milltown, I suppose that was never going to be allowed to stand.

My mother was born in the townland of Parkroe, about a mile from Milltown. It is a tiny place, on a road that turns left off the N17 before rejoining it about a hundred metres away from the village's welcome sign. So it describes a fairly perfect semi-circle, around which were houses and farms that had been built in the early 1800s.

When she was growing up, one of her neighbours was Johnny Connolly, who in time would move out onto the main road and become next-door neighbour to my mother and father when they built their house. He was a lovely neighbour, and a beautiful person – the only visitor who ever called to our house via the back door, not the front.

I had a recollection that Johnny was a great man for the hurling, despite his diminutive size, and I always presumed that if there was hurling in Milltown it was unorganized, impromptu and informal, with fellas like Johnny at its heart. I could imagine games in Parkroe between neighbours, and I could imagine my uncles Noel and Jim being stuck in the middle of it as kids. But real games – with a referee, jerseys, two sets of goalposts? That was hard to imagine. Nevertheless, there it was, in black and white, in the *Tuam Herald*.

Jim sent me a photograph of a Milltown hurling reunion, taken in the early 1980s, long after the demise of the Michael Davitts hurling club. Among the men pictured were neighbours I recognized instantly, who I would never in a million years have guessed were hurlers. What possessed them?

Some of them were decent footballers too, but many more were lads I'd never really had chalked down as big supporters of the club . . . and by that I mean the Gaelic football club.

There was one man, seated in the centre of the front row, with a dark tan, white trousers and dark jacket. I presumed he must have flown home from America for this reunion, because he looked extraordinarily dapper, in a way that Irish men in the 1980s quite simply never did. This, it turned out, was Pat Heaney.

Everyone called him Scadán. Culkin's Hill, where he lived, is the only elevation of any kind in the village, and so the single tree at its modest summit is visible for miles around. I might have searched for years to find a man who would more perfectly embody the uphill struggle of hurling against the headwinds of history and football. Here was the sort of man who would refuse a lift in my father's minibus to Croke Park on the morning of a game, instead preferring to cycle the 130 miles himself. Is this the only kind of person who would think to try to implant hurling in a football-mad place like Milltown?

I did some further digging, and discovered another article from the *Tuam Herald*, this one from May 1958.

> An allegation that efforts to establish hurling in the Milltown area were prevented because 'football was a money spinner' was made at the Connacht Council G. A. A. meeting in Castlerea on Thursday last by Mr. P. G. Heaney, of Devon House, Belmont, Milltown.
>
> He brought an appeal against a decision of the Galway County Board refusing to accept an affiliation for a hurling club in Milltown. In his appeal, Mr. Heaney said that last year he was refused 'because the existing (football) club in

the parish objected', but was given encouragement to apply this year.

He was refused in 1956 because 'it was late in the year' when the case was heard, and told he could apply in 1957 . . . Mr. Heaney, speaking on his appeal, said that three years ago there were a few groups playing hurling in the parish. Seeing the possibility of forming a parish hurling team, he brought his group to Milltown and arranged a challenge game. They attended the annual meeting of the football club and asked 'what they were going to do' about hurling but 'were abused'. In March, the football club sent in a list of hurlers and registered them as a hurling team.

'The following year the North Galway Board accepted our affiliation,' he continued, 'but when Milltown football club objected at the next meeting they rescinded their decision. We appealed to Galway County Board, who ruled that our affiliation should not have been accepted. The following year our affiliation was again refused . . . The explanation as to why Galway County Board is down on us is because football is a money spinner.'

Chairman: Better stick to the case.

Mr. Heaney: You must hear the background. I will stand any investigation.

Mr. Nestor: I am not going to sit here and let members of Galway County Board be slandered.

Mr. Heaney: The G. A. A. is democratic. We want to see hurling fostered in the parish.

Mr. Nestor: There is a hurling team and they took part in the League and Championship.

Chairman: If you have a hurling team, what is to stop you from fostering hurling?

Mr. Heaney: You don't want to build up a thing for someone else to knock it down. The North Galway Board will take up all the Sundays with football.

Mr. M. Cox (Roscommon) said that it seemed that relations between the football club and this gentleman are not good.

Mr. Heaney: At the annual meeting the secretary of the football club said it was a step in the wrong direction as Milltown was a predominantly football area.

Chairman: If you and a few others are so anxious, why don't you and a few others try to get them to affiliate a hurling club and carry on hurling? Mr. Heaney summed up the whole thing when he said he would not go into that and let somebody else get the whole credit.

Mr. J. Dunne: In 1956 this man appealed to the County Board. They summoned the chairman and secretary of Milltown club who said they invited Mr. Heaney to take officership in the club but they would not let him run hurling on his own. Last year they took part in the championship and Mr. Heaney did not assist them. He won't be allowed to run the club on his own.

Mr. Heaney: I was not offered officership in the club.

The article finishes with a rapid-fire blast of dialogue that is dramaturgy of the highest quality.

Mr. Cox: This is a matter for Milltown parish.
   Mr. J. J. Fahy: If they are good Gaels they will settle it.
   Mr. Dunne: If he throws in his lot, it will settle it all.
   Mr. Nestor: We were told you would not cooperate.
   Mr. Heaney: The North Galway Board don't want to encourage hurling, as football is too strong thanks to Sean Purcell and men like him.
   Chairman: The appeal is lost.

When Scadán quotes a football club executive who said a hurling club 'was a step in the wrong direction as Milltown was a predominantly football area', it rings true to me, and would ring true to many other people who come from places like Milltown.

Whether he was abused at an annual general meeting of the GAA club, as he alleges here, is open to interpretation, because it is impossible to read this article and not also come to the conclusion that Scadán was an incredibly difficult man to deal with. He appears to have been keenly attuned to any slight, and distrustful of anyone who seemed eager to bring this situation to some kind of resolution. What hurling in Milltown needed, it appears, was a softly-softly approach – an attempt to show that hurling was no threat to football, just a worthwhile addition to the

Gaelic games offering in the village. It is clear that there were people in the parish who were very interested in hurling, and were glad of the opportunity to play the game. But Scadán was not a man who did softly-softly, as one of his few surviving teammates from that time would tell me.

Padraic Godwin was a very fine footballer in his day, and I played senior football for Milltown for years with his sons Eoin and Terence. His grandsons are playing football with Milltown now, and into his eighty-eighth year he keeps a wonderful home in the far end of the village, as far away from my house as you can be and still be in the parish.

I hadn't been in his house for years, and when I sat down in his kitchen, I realized his front window looked straight out onto Culkin's Hill. Scadán had been a neighbour. I told Padraic I'd never climbed to the top of the hill, and he asked me if I knew what kind of tree it was that stood alone at the summit. I didn't. 'An ash tree, of course.'

When I asked him where Scadán's love of hurling came from, he suggested that he must've picked it up when he went to teacher-training college, which he left before he graduated.

'There was a bit of a rebel in him . . . but sure there was a bit of a rebel in all of us that played that time.' And this was something I had wondered about – there weren't that many dual players, apart from Padraic and another man, Paddy Forde, both of whom would have been among the most committed football men in the parish at that time.

Many of the other men in that photo from the early 1980s, as I've said, were not people I'd have pegged as natural hurlers. There was an element, it appeared, that the hurling club was an outlet for people who might not have been too bothered about the newly formed football club, which had only been in existence since 1953. Before that, footballers from the village played with Dunmore or other neighbouring parishes. Having only just founded a football club of their own, they surely looked on hurling as an unnecessary complication to a club that had barely established itself. If there were personality clashes, as there inevitably were, then hurling offered a route to play a bit of sport. And if Scadán was intemperate, then there may well have been a similar level of obduracy on the football side of things.

Even so, there are indications that the two codes in Milltown were not entirely hostile to one another. Padraic remembers playing a hurling match, followed immediately by a football game, in the same field in the village, and the teams wore the same jerseys for both codes. But we cannot attribute the fact that hurling withered on the vine in Milltown purely to personality clashes. Hurling was an inconvenience in Milltown back then, and it would probably be seen as an inconvenience today too, if a similarly single-minded individual decided to pick up Scadán's baton and run with it. The Gaelic football club is fighting the headwinds of rural depopulation, trying to compete against Galway city and commuter-belt clubs that are experiencing an explosion in population numbers. If you have only a limited number of hours on the pitch with the kids in your catchment area, the question would very quickly be asked – why would you halve that coaching time again, just to offer them hurling?

So why is Gaelic football so much more popular, nationally, than hurling? The reasons, after careful consideration of 140 years of the GAA, can be summed up in two words – ease and economics. Gaelic football is a much easier game to play as well as being much, much cheaper. And at various times in the history of the GAA, when the association was growing rapidly, the Irish economy was on its knees. In the 1880s, Ireland was dirt-poor. To play a football game required only one football. Hurling required a minimum of thirty finely honed pieces of ash. This stuff mattered.

Beyond the price of raw materials there was a deeper economic force at play. Farm labouring was cruel, thankless work. The worse your land, the harder you had to work to make it pay, and the less time you had to be devoting to your hurling skills, or to any other leisure activity for that matter. It is no coincidence that hurling's heartlands are the best farmland in the country.

In an essay from the early 1990s titled 'The Geography

of Hurling', the historian Kevin Whelan writes of this economic disparity between hurling and football areas:

> In almost every case, that boundary divides big farm and small farm areas and marks the transition from fertile, drift-covered limestone lowland to hillier, hungrier, wetter shales, flagstones, grits and granites. In County Galway, for example, hurling has not put down roots in the bony granite outcrops of Connemara, and in Clare the poorly drained flagstone deposits are equally inhospitable. If ash is emblematic of hurling areas, the rush is the distinctive symbol of football territory.

The idea of reviving hurling was what got Michael Cusack out to the Phoenix Park in January of 1884. The mythology of hurling was strong enough to allow its founders to link it to Irish ideas of nationhood and patriotism. But as early as 1886, the first great GAA journalist – P. P. Sutton, a Wexford hurler who only tolerated football – was already asking himself the question: what can be done to help the spread of hurling in the weaker counties? He even used the phrase 'weaker counties'!

But notwithstanding the failure of Michael Davitts hurling club, and the underlying economic and topographical distinction between hurling country and football country, hurling was and remains part of the consciousness of Milltown and other places like it. There was Micheál Ó hÉithir, for a start, who made heroes of hurlers, to people who'd never even seen the game in the flesh. The romance of the dust rising in the parallelogram as he chronicled the exploits of Ring and Mackey is hard to quantify for a modern audience, but when historians talk of Ó hÉithir as being just about as influential a figure as the GAA has ever seen, it's not hyperbole. He was succeeded on radio in time by Mícheál Ó Muircheartaigh, whose audition for a radio commentating gig, a couple of weeks after he came up from Kerry to Dublin for teaching-training college, was a hurling game in Croke Park. That also happened to be the first game of hurling he'd ever seen in the flesh – a remarkable fact in itself.

The car radio on the beach broadcasting a hurling game from Thurles is still a particularly vivid childhood memory for people my age. Too often now, commentary on hurling descends into a kind of pastiche of Ó hÉithir and Ó Muircheartaigh in full flow, but it remains a thrilling sport to listen to on the radio. And you certainly don't have to be a hurling fan to have enjoyed analysts like Cyril Farrell and Ger Loughnane, or latterly Anthony Daly and John Mullane. The game has a unique ability to generate spokespeople who are knowledgeable, passionate or entertaining, or all three at once. The game is king, and while they, and plenty of others besides, might all have healthy personal egos, it is all in service to the game. Their love for their sport transcends everything else.

Hurling existed elsewhere in the culture of the country too, in a way that Gaelic football just didn't. In the house that I grew up in was a book called *Glenanaar* by Canon Patrick Sheehan, a priest in County Cork who sold novels by the bucketload throughout the early years of the twentieth century. My mother had been given it by her primary-school teacher, and she and Jim both remembered the book mainly for the thrilling nature of the hurling scenes in it.

I read it for the first time before I left for Waterford. It is very much a work of its time. But the descriptions of a hurling game in the opening twenty pages are terrific.

The novel begins with the arrival into the town of a mysterious 'Yank', about whom little or nothing is known. We can surely all agree that 'He suddenly appeared in our village street, gorgeous, and caparisoned from head to heel in all kinds of sartorial splendour' is a magnificent opening sentence.

As can be expected, how and why 'the Yank' came to be in the town is the topic of fevered conversation, which soon turns to outright anger at the newcomer's refusal to explain himself. A couple of weeks into his stay in the village of Doneraile (where all Canon Sheehan's books are set), a county final is being played.

> It was a Sunday afternoon in the late summer . . . It was a big affair . . . the final 'try' for the County championship between

the Cork 'Shandons' and our own brave 'Skirmishers'. There was a mighty crowd assembled. Sidecars, wagonettes, traps of every shape and hue and form, from the farmer's cart with the heavy quilt to the smart buggy of the merchant, brought in all the afternoon a great concourse of people . . . We are no Sabbatarians in Ireland. Neither are we quite depleted yet. It would surprise any one familiar with all the modern, doleful jeremiads about the depopulation of Ireland to see such a smartly dressed, intelligent crowd in a country village. And if he had any misgivings or doubts about the physique and pluck of 'the fighting race', he had only to stand still, when the athletes stripped for the contest, and see in those clean-cut, well-built figures the nerve and muscle that go to build up an energetic and pushing race.

You get the picture.

At three o'clock the teams were called to their places by their respective captains. There was a brief consultation with the referee, a coin was flung into the air, sides were taken, the winners turning their backs to the wind, and in a moment, one could only see that ball tossed hither and thither in the struggle, and a confused mass of men and camans, as they fought fiercely for victory and the tide of the battle rolled uncertain here and there across the field . . .

Not a word broke from that whirling mass as the heavy ball leaped hither and thither, tossed by the camans from hand to hand, or rolled swiftly over the level grass, as some young athlete, with the fleetness of a deer, tapped it on before him... You heard only the patter of the feet, the light or heavy tap-tap-tap on the ball, the crack of the camans as they crossed in the air above or on the grass beneath; and now and again the screams of women and girls, who stampeded wildly when the ball was driven into their midst.

The Skirmishers of Doneraile are within touching distance of victory when they lose their captain to a bout of illness.

They held a long and eager consultation; and finally decided to enlist one or other of the spectators, who had been members of the Club, but not listed men. These shook their heads. The issue was too important. They would not take the responsibility. Five o'clock was near; and the referee was about to give his final decision in favour of the strangers, when, to the astonishment of everyone, 'the Yank', throwing away a half-burned cigar, and calmly divesting himself of coat and waist-coat, which he carefully rolled up and placed in the hands of a spectator, came forward, took up a caman, tested it, as if it were a Toledo blade, by leaning all his weight on it, and said in an accent of cool indifference:

'Let me take a hand: I guess I can manage it.'

You can probably tell where this is going.

The ball was once more tossed high, the victory swayed from one side to the other; the cheers rose wildly and voluminously from the adherents of both teams; until, at last, the 'Shandons', pressing home for victory, drove the ball right under 'the Yank's' legs. The foremost champion, rushing forward to get it through the goal, found himself, he knew not how, about twenty feet away from the ball; and then it seemed as if a cyclone had struck the field. At least, a straight path was cut through the swaying, confused mass of the combatants, who in some mysterious way yielded right and left. Disregarding all modern rules and regulations, 'the Yank' had struck straight before him; and with his powerful arms and shoulders had cut his way clean as a swathe of ripe corn is levelled by the teeth of a mowing-machine in the early harvest time.

A few cries of 'A foul! A foul!' were raised; but they were hushed into ignominious silence by the plaudits of the crowd . . . the whole mad tumult culminated in a wild Irish cheer, as the ball flew swiftly over the heads of the rival combatants, and, despite the frantic efforts of the goalkeeper on the Shandons' side, passed out gaily through the gates of the goal.

Obviously much of this evokes Kickham's 'the pride of the little village', but I can see how my mam and Jim could be swept up by it all. The game sounds chaotic and wonderful, and the emotions created are brilliantly, dramatically evoked . . . even if it could charitably be said that Canon Sheehan was not a man with a gift for brevity or understatement (who would dare edit a man of God?).

These are minor quibbles, delivered over a century after the words were written. I enjoyed it immensely, this tale of the mystery man who had just arrived in town, delivered the goods, and won the acclaim of his new neighbours.

I mean, why wouldn't I like the sound of that?

4

With the transfer taken care of, and my addition to the team WhatsApp group rubber-stamped, it was time for me to move in with John and his wife Marian. Gill would follow at the end of the school year, on 1 June.

John and Marian lived in the house where my father had grown up, and it was where my grandmother had lived until her death in 2004, so it was a home full of memories. It was then, as it is now, a bustling hub of activity, all revolving around John and his attendant cast of characters, including but not limited to those of the animal kingdom. He had three dogs, including one called Derek (given to him for free, by a man named Derek, under the proviso that John must name it after him), and his rather portly, unsightly, but nevertheless extremely charismatic Shetland pony Seamus, who does valuable work across the breeding sheds of west Waterford as a pint-sized teaser horse.

At one stage in the not-too-distant past, John walked

a couple of hundred metres every morning to attend to a neighbour's farm, and he would be followed on that short journey by a cat and three hens, walking in single file behind him. No one really had an answer as to how this was possible. But it was John, and so nothing really felt impossible.

There was also a seemingly non-stop stream of people calling in for a chat – fellow farmers, horsey types, local businessmen, GAA heads. Stand still in John's house and you'd meet the whole parish, apparently. After a few days of this speed-integration into the community, there was nothing else for it but to prepare for my first training session.

And there was much to take care of. My first port of call was a sports shop, to pick up socks and shorts in the Old Parish colours of white and red. I needed a new pair of boots, as the last pair of 'soft ground' football boots I'd bought were starting to show signs of wear and tear (I had an exposed view of a toe, which was not in the manufacturer's original design). I didn't want to show up to my first ever training session looking like a fella who couldn't even take care of his own footwear. But did I want to show up looking like a fella who had just bought a new pair of boots especially for a run-of-the-mill training session in early April? I thought I'd like a glove, because I could remember an evening spent in the Phoenix Park with Collie and Mark, playing D-O-N-K-E-Y and hitting sliotars back and forth to each other for an hour until it felt like my hand was completely smashed to pieces. But a glove also seemed to carry troubling connotations – a suggestion that I wasn't tough enough for this sport. Being tough enough for this sport was something I most certainly was not, but I didn't want my teammates to discover that just yet.

I went in search of a helmet. I wanted to be able to browse the various makes, models, and colours to find my dream-head protection. But when I got down to it, I hadn't a clue what I was looking for. I texted my friend Jamie Wall, the 2024 Fitzgibbon Cup-winning manager of Mary Immaculate College, in search of answers. 'What's new and HOT in hurling helmet style? Is there one make in particular that's so hot right now? I want the Cadillac of hurling helmets.'

I gave him my aesthetic judgements on some of the makes I was browsing at that exact moment. One brand seemed quite hip, but I was informed it was 'also liable to leave you with brain fragments left on the field if you get a smack. And let's face it, the chances of that increase exponentially at the level you will be playing.'

I decided to move on to colour scheme. What was the etiquette when it came to closely matching up with your club's own colours? Old Parish's jersey is red, therefore . . . a red helmet? Apparently this is a major no-no. You'd look like a raving psychopath if you showed up head to toe in your club colours. Your helmet colour is a chance for you to break free from the constraints of history and village tradition. So blue it would be: the colour of Milltown and, for the most part, of Templeogue Synge Street.

I went into one shop, which had a decent selection of Mycro, the brand I'd decided to go with after lengthy consultation with Jamie, but none in blue. I spent an hour trying helmets on for size – it appeared my head was merely large, not extra-large as I'd presumed – before slinking home empty-handed.

The following morning, just hours before my first training session, I spent another ninety minutes looking for a blue fucking helmet. Eventually I gave up and bought a large Mycro in red in an Elverys sports shop somewhere in Waterford city centre. If buying a hurling helmet that matches your club jersey is a sin, then at this point I was willing to be guilty. I also searched for a right-hand protective glove – my right hand being the one most in need of protection, as I hold my hurley in my left and catch with my right. But, worryingly, the only gloves for sale appeared to be kids' sizes. My initial fears around what the wearing of a glove would say about me might have been correct.

I had my dear old hurley, but it needed to be retaped, and I didn't have the slightest idea how to do that. I knew, too, that I needed to prepare myself mentally for the likelihood that my hurley would be smashed into a thousand pieces within the first five minutes of my first training session.

I was planning to go to a specialist hurley-maker and get a genuine, game-ready piece, but for my first session I was going to need a spare. In Elverys I ended up buying one that, appropriately, looked like something you'd buy in a sporting megastore. The hurley I'd been using for the last two years is a 34-inch, and I definitely didn't want one any longer than that. I went for a 33-inch instead, so that when the time came for me to order a new batch I'd know which size I preferred.

I thought I'd get a rush of excitement from buying the various accoutrements that fill up a hurler's gear-bag, but there was something about my brand-new helmet and my store-bought pristine hurley that grimmed me out a little. I felt like the guy who has all the gear in the gym but doesn't have a clue what he's doing. Of course, this feeling was correct. I really didn't know what I was doing.

I was even stressing out a little about what to wear to training. I decided that the brand-new red socks and white shorts that I'd bought last week would make me look like a maniac – like I was trying too hard – so I went through my GAA gear selection, digging out the most worn-looking items of clothing in the Templeogue Synge Street colours.

Once that was done, I sat down to watch the national hurling league final on TV. Early on, watching Billy Ryan score a point for Kilkenny, a thought struck me: he hit that ball while running at full pace. I had never hit a ball on the run in my life. I'd been doing all my striking basically standing still. This was daunting to contemplate. Nevertheless, as the match went on, I started feeling giddy. The fact that sixteen hours after this game finished I would be playing hurling myself, with actual hurlers, made it completely different from every other game of hurling I'd ever watched.

I was up early, and I was a little nervous – so I togged out and went into Dungarvan for a pre-session coffee. As I was walking to my preferred coffee shop on the square, an old man stared me down for ten seconds before he said, 'You'll win handy today.' What the hell was this lad talking about? Then I realized: I was wearing Tipperary colours. Tipperary were in town to play Waterford in the Munster senior football championship. If I could plausibly pass for a Tipperary footballer, then football in Tipp was even more screwed than I thought.

I drank my coffee and then, as I was walking back to my car, I was accosted by a Second Captains listener. I was not overly eager to broadcast my move on the show, or anywhere else for that matter, and so had kept a dignified silence about my new living arrangements. I was not comfortable with the idea that some maniac might decide to come and watch the early days of my humiliation. So how could I explain why I was togged out for training on a Sunday morning in west Waterford? As it turned out, I didn't have to. The guy already knew I had moved down, courtesy of the local grapevine.

These two interactions rattled me, for reasons I couldn't quite put my finger on.

Two minutes later, I had barely started the car when my cousin Bríd rang to tell me I'd been spotted in Dungarvan. She reiterated her invitation for me to join the An Rinn under-8 camogie team she coaches, which she felt would be a more welcoming first step into the hurling world. 'I don't need this,' I told her.

The road out from Dungarvan is the N25 from Waterford to Cork, which runs along the coast of the bay for about two kilometres before snaking its way up a steep incline and levelling out about 150 metres above sea level. At the foot of that incline is the turn-off for Helvick Head, the area known as Gaeltacht na nDéise, the Waterford Gaeltacht. That road runs up and along the side of the elevation that stretches out east from Dungarvan along the length of the peninsula. About two kilometres in, the road forks. The low road leads down to the village of An Rinn at sea level, with its Gaeltacht college, two pubs, and a beautiful swimming cove just metres from the pier at Helvick. The high road off that fork leads to An Sean Phobal – Old Parish.

On the high road, you rise precipitously to stunning views of Dungarvan Bay and along the entire coast of the county of Waterford. The road then levels out and brings you straight to the village, such as it is. There is a pub at a crossroads, called John Paul's, and about a hundred metres after John Paul's is a small development of houses, a naíonra (pre-school) and national school, followed by a church and graveyard, which also contains the Halla Colmán, the community centre. If you'd turned right at the crossroads at John Paul's, within a hundred metres you'd have encountered the house my father was born in. If you'd turned left and gone a similar distance, that would lead you down to the GAA pitch, Páirc Colmáin.

St Colman had a monastery in Old Parish, and it was he who baptized St Declan of Ardmore – the man who Christianized Waterford before the arrival of St Patrick to Ireland. Old Parish is so called because local lore proclaims it to be Ireland's oldest Christian parish – An Sean Phobal.

I was twenty-five minutes early for training. It afforded me an opportunity to meet the manager, Sean Wade, before any other players arrived. I had texted Sean once or twice, and was now eager to reiterate to him how new to all this I was. He told me it was fine, John had told him of my limitations, and even though he took everything John said to him with a pinch of salt, he understood completely. I thought further elaboration on my deficiencies would seem like over-egging it, so I left it at that.

Sean took me on a quick tour of the clubhouse, which used to be the local creamery. My father and his brothers used to deliver milk here in twenty-gallon churns on horse and cart throughout their childhood. Sean's dad Maurice and my father were in school together, and upstairs in the committee room there's a photo of Dad and the rest of the 1968 West Waterford junior football championship-winning team on the wall.

The same photograph hangs in our house in Milltown. And it's the same photo I saw years and years ago in John Paul's pub, halfway between the GAA pitch and Dad's old home. I was twenty-three or twenty-four at the time, and couldn't believe the likeness between myself at that age and Dad at the age of twenty.

Looking at that photo, in a place I barely knew and felt like a tourist in, was disconcertingly like looking in a mirror. With ten minutes to go until my first ever hurling training session, 160 kilometres from Galway and the same distance from my new home in Dublin, the thought struck me that this day might have been inevitable since that moment, but I shook it off.

By the time the tour was finished, my uncle John had arrived, and so too had the club chairman, my dad's first cousin Michael Hogan. He immediately asked me what size shorts I wore: he couldn't be having me in Tipperary colours. I started to explain my unease at appearing at my first training session with a new helmet, a new (spare) hurley, a brand-new pair of socks and a brand-new pair of shorts, but decided I'd already spent enough time obsessing over that without involving Michael in my neuroses.

The first player arrived about ten minutes later, and we began to puck around, along with one of the selectors. I could feel the eyes of my uncle and Michael boring into me. One swing off my right side dribbled along the ground, but other than that I was able to at least hit the ball out of my way, even if no one would be calling me the sweetest striker of a sliotar they'd ever seen.

Nearly every player that arrived came over to shake my hand and welcome me personally. One of them, I realized with a shock, was a blood relative: Michael's nephew Cathal, my second cousin. I felt like I'd be happy to stay there forever, pucking the ball back and forth absent-mindedly as I'd always done any time I'd ever picked up a hurl. But today was different.

The whistle blew and the group formed itself around Sean. First off, he welcomed me to the squad. He explained that I was a football man, new to hurling, but that I was most welcome and ready to contribute. He also mentioned, as he had done in his opening message in the WhatsApp group, the long-standing involvement of my family in the club, including the fact that my father and my uncle Deaglán had played in the 1960s and 1970s. In the way of GAA clubs, the fact that that was fifty years ago didn't matter. Most of my teammates' fathers had played for the club too. I might never have met any of them before, but that link was enough. Sean's introduction was perfectly pitched, and I felt a great gust of relief that all of my painstaking expectation-management over the course of the previous month or so (*I've never played! I'd never owned a helmet until twenty-four hours ago! I'm possibly a danger to myself and others!*) had had some effect.

Then my uncle opened his mouth. John had hung around the players' huddle, in the way that club grandees are allowed to do, and then declared over the top of Sean: 'Don't be surprised, lads, if he's great. It's just in his nature to be good, he's a Murphy – that'll just be the nature breaking out in him.'

The players erupted in laughter, and I saw that my main problem for this summer would be keeping my uncle from cracking everyone up any time I did anything.

The session began with some runs and stretches, and I was glad of the feeling of familiarity this granted me. As we stretched our hammers and our quads and our glutes, I could nearly convince myself that this was well-trodden ground. But that feeling was never going to last long.

We were training on the club's small astroturf pitch – about forty-five metres by twenty-five metres – because the weather had been brutal for the past few months, and we were saving the grass pitch. We broke into two groups and started the session with a routine where each player took the ball on the run, ran out fifteen metres or so, and then turned to drill a pass along the ground to the next man in line. The bounce off the artificial grass was reliable, but it was super-fast, and it was a great challenge for your first touch. Having established that the man in front of me was called Ciarán Ó Mathúna, I got my bas behind the first ball he hit at me, but it just rolled all the way up the hurley and out over my right shoulder. When I finally got it into my hand, I soloed to the other end and delivered a reasonably accurate but rather watery pass to the next man running on. The next ball Ciarán put my way was hit noticeably more gently, and I appreciated it.

Then we added a little change-up – instead of drilling the ball along the ground back in the direction you just ran, you hand-passed it to the man charging onto it. I realized, as I waited my turn, that I'd never hit a hand-pass to a moving target before. My first effort duly flew way over the head of the onrushing player.

The next change-up saw us not passing the ball along the ground but firing it through the air – 'at the fella's face-guard', as Sean helpfully put it. Ciarán duly fired one at my head, and I stuck my hand up to catch it. Even as I was congratulating myself for the catch, the ball bounced out of my hand. Same with the next one. The third one (all three passes had been perfectly placed) I finally held on to, and the sting of the ball into my palm was quite pleasurable.

The passes I was hitting were weak in comparison to the passes I was receiving, but they were at least travelling.

I felt I wasn't entirely useless – that I was not actively harming the session.

The next drill had most of the players at the south-east corner of the pitch, with one man stationed at every other corner. The name of the game here was to hand-pass the ball to the man at every corner and take it back off him, all at high speed, while being pursued by another man. Once you turned the last corner, you head off for goal, and the man behind you is trying to hook you.

On the first go-round, I fluffed my hand-passes and never even got a chance to advance on the keeper. The second time, I got a beaut of a pass from the last man on the corner, and I set off for goal at high speed. As I approached the goal, I threw the ball up and prepared to see the net bulge. But then I got hooked by my pursuer, and my swing at the ball barely made contact.

Getting hooked is like getting your pocket picked. It's entirely different from getting your shot blocked down in Gaelic football (or soccer or rugby for that matter). In those sports, you are never going to get blocked by an opponent who is completely invisible to you. When you see a defender coming in for a block, you can attempt to take some remedial action.

But if you're out hurling for the first time, and wearing a helmet for the first time, then the hook comes completely out of nowhere. I'd seen plenty of county players anticipate the hook, but I had no conception of how they did it. In this drill, I knew that there was someone behind me, but I had no idea whether he was a metre or ten metres back. I certainly thought that someone was going to have to *feel* a lot closer to me than it turned out was required. I swung, I missed, and I was just left staring at the ball dribbling pathetically towards the goalkeeper.

The session continued in this vein for a while, and then we broke into two teams and played a rather frenetic game of nine on nine, on a very small pitch, where I was utterly lost. And that was that. It had been unbelievably enjoyable, and the warmth of the welcome rather shocked me. I hadn't been preparing myself for outright hostility, but I'd anticipated an element of standoffishness. Instead, and I suppose I should credit my uncle here, it had been a beautiful way to spend a Sunday morning.

John was beaming: 'Jesus, you're flying it, lad.' He has a penchant for exaggeration, but what this meant was that he could hold his head high for this weekend at least.

And I supposed I could too.

The following day, I headed off to Scotland for a four-day driving holiday with my brother Paul and my father. Dad was anxious to hear all about my new teammates, but there were no more than three or four first-name-and-surname combinations I was entirely sure of, and another ten first names I could be reasonably certain about. Beyond that, I had no information that he could actually use.

'Are there any Terrys playing? Any Frenches? Any Powers?' I wasn't sure, as most of the lads only attached their first names to their WhatsApp numbers, but we had some fun trying to fill in the blanks. I was feeling very good about things, as Paul and I drove through the Highlands towards Skye. We were bouncing from place to place, staying in B&Bs and hotels.

One night, after Dad went to bed, Paul and I discussed my hurling plans for the summer. Paul was the public relations officer for St Mary's GAA club in Athenry. They are historically one of Galway's most successful hurling clubs, and Paul is surrounded on all sides by Hurling Men of unimpeachable reputation. He is under no illusion that he will ever be considered as such himself, even if his son is one of the most promising young hurlers in the club.

With the help of some whiskey, I felt sufficiently emboldened to tell him that I thought this hurling craic was actually going to be pretty simple. What a disaster it would be for my book, I mused aloud, if I could so easily master this famously difficult sport?

Paul has never been a man to mince his words, and he wasn't about to start now. 'I saw the Athenry Junior E team win a county final last year. They were all about your age, they had all won county senior medals, and they were all very, very good hurlers. By no means did they walk away with that championship. And that's a couple of levels below the level you'll be playing at. If you avoid devastating injury it'll be a miracle, you absolute lunatic.'

I chalked it up as yet another example of Paul's trademark pessimism. You should have seen me at training! I could lift, I could strike, I could hand-pass . . . more or less.

'It's on an astroturf, and five minutes before you did all that, the team manager told everyone you'd never hurled before. It's hardly laboratory conditions to prove you're an actual hurler, is it?'

Hmmm. I was willing to concede that he might have a point.

I was back for training the following weekend, having missed only one session while I was in Scotland, and we were once again on the astroturf because (the Sunday morning sunshine notwithstanding) the weather had continued to be awful in my absence.

Sean had taken the session himself the week before, but this week the team's regular coach, Tadhg Murphy, was there, and since I was the first man at training again I had time to introduce myself to him.

He's a Corkman, with the upbeat, confident bearing of many from that part of the world. I found out later that he won All-Ireland minor titles in hurling and football and an All-Ireland colleges hurling medal with Farranferris all in the same year, 1974. That's three All-Ireland titles in six months, as a teenager, which is a pretty astonishing achievement. He went on to win an All-Ireland senior hurling medal for Cork. He also got one of the most famous scores in the history of Cork football, when his last-minute goal beat Kerry in the 1983 Munster senior football final, for Cork's first provincial title in nine years. That happened ten months after Seamus Darby had done something similar for Offaly in the last minute of the All-Ireland final, denying Kerry the five-in-a-row. If Darby's goal is the most famous moment in the history of Gaelic football, it's still only in the ha'penny place in Cork compared to Tadhg's.

He had a house in Ardmore, only a couple of miles over, and so he had been roped in a few years before to help out, and had ended up coaching the Old Parish hurlers to three West Waterford titles in a row, and the previous year's county Junior C championship. It's no exaggeration to say that he had revolutionized hurling in the club.

I started knocking around with John Flynn, who good-naturedly talked down his hurling ability while demonstrating in an easy, no-frills way the touch and the skill that made him one of the best players in the club.

Once the session was underway, Tadhg ran his orders and moved us briskly from drill to drill. Two sessions in, and it was clear already that 75 per cent of hurling training consists of getting your first touch sharp, and then keeping it sharp. This is as it must be: the game revolves around whether you can get the ball in your hand first time. It was a searching examination, and I was coming up short repeatedly.

After a while we broke into two groups, one with bibs and one without. At either end of the astroturf, there was an equal number of bibs and non-bibs. The name of the game if you had a bib on was to try to win possession at your end, and then find a moving target in a bib at the other end. So the skills being worked on were clever movement to get some separation from your marker, winning possession, and then the ability to hit a twenty-five-metre stick-pass to a man on the move up the other end.

In this drill, I found that my experience of inside-forward movement in football was at least vaguely helpful. But it was all for nothing: any time the ball came my way, I was incapable of corralling it.

We finished with a game, and this week it was more like seven-a-side. Late on, John Flynn (an absolute unit) came charging through the middle on the hunt for a winning goal. Out of nowhere came another player (also an absolute unit) who body-slammed him and pulled across him with his hurley simultaneously. It was exactly the sort of tackle that would usually cause a riot in a training session – or at least it would have done in Templeogue Synge Street.

John was down on his hunkers, and we called the session off. As we were walking to the huddle, I kept a beady eye on the two combatants, still unsure how this was going to end. Sean turned to the group and said, 'Imagine what they'd do to each other if they weren't brothers.' I shouldn't have been surprised. Of course they were brothers! It's the first rule of country clubs. I felt at home already.

At the end of the session we were informed that the Waterford County Board had set a fixture for the following weekend . . . a football league fixture. My career as a dual player was about to begin.

5

For much of its history, Old Parish was solely a Gaelic football club. Its enthusiastic embrace of hurling in more recent times is emblematic of the growth of the game in west Waterford.

My father played much more football than hurling for Old Parish in the 1960s, although I was informed by Declan Terry, another one of the club grandees, of one particularly memorable occasion when they were short of both hurlers and hurleys, and Dad was prevailed upon to play.

At the exact moment before throw-in when the An Sean Phobal team were being informed that they only had fifteen hurleys and that they should try to make sure not to break any of them, Dad was testing the mettle of the one he'd just been handed. He put his weight on it to gauge its suppleness . . . and, of course, snapped it in two. He had to play with whatever was left.

Hurling wasn't even an option for Michael Hogan when

he came along as the best footballer in the club in the mid-1970s. He never played a game of hurling in his life, as Old Parish was solely a football club for the entire length of his club career. Anyone who was interested in hurling could wander off and play for An Rinn, but it wasn't done too often. Many of the club elders, my uncle John included, loved watching hurling, but would still call themselves football people at heart.

The greatest success the club ever had was winning the county junior football championship in 1949, which got them promoted to senior. That was the only time the club had competed at the top grade. Their nickname was 'The Shocks', and I had always been a little curious as to just how that had come about. I heard a number of possibilities aired — one was that this success of the men of '49 was happening at around the time of rural electrification, and getting hit by a member of the An Sean Phobal team was said to be roughly as comfortable as getting an electric shock. This was certainly the most fun explanation I had heard, so I was happy to go with that. The club has a little lightning bolt on its crest, dramatically striking the top of the lighthouse at the bottom of the parish, Mine Head.

In fact, hurling only made a comeback in Old Parish in the past five years, and it came about in large part because of the influence of another football man, Liam Ó Lonáin. Liam had played for the Waterford footballers for years – years when the county's hurlers were becoming among the best-loved GAA teams of all time. He was also a very fine hurler with An Rinn, and he did untold work in the national school, teaching the kids Gaelic football and hurling.

Those young lads were able to play hurling under age for the An Gaeltacht club, which due to a lack of playing numbers has been a long-running amalgamation between An Rinn and An Sean Phobal solely at underage level, and they were very successful. But the lads didn't want to play hurling for An Rinn, they wanted to represent where they were from, and that meant restarting the on-again, off-again adult hurling wing of Old Parish GAA club. They entered the West Waterford Junior C championship in 2021, they found Tadhg in his holiday home in Ardmore, and they set to work.

These lads' desire to play hurling was only natural. They had grown up in a world where their county was regularly competing for national honours. Waterford had already been to three All-Ireland finals in their lifetime (having reached only five in the entire twentieth century). As kids they didn't have to look outside the county for heroes – they were meeting Dan Shanahan and Jamie Barron and Michael 'Brick' Walsh at club games and county games for their entire lives.

If you're good enough to make a county under-14 development squad, the potential for you to play representative hurling at the top county level is within touching distance. Waterford teams don't even have to be making All-Ireland finals – even competing in the Munster championship is about as glamorous, as challenging, as unpredictable, and as exciting as being a sportsperson in Ireland gets. By contrast, playing inter-county football for Waterford is a less thrilling proposition: it is perennially one of the weakest football counties in the country.

If you look at the Waterford team that started their last game in the 2024 Munster hurling championship, you'll find five players from the city and surrounding clubs, with ten from the west of the county. This would have been unheard of at any other stage in Waterford's hurling history, but it has been building for a couple of decades now. Waterford won possibly the greatest Munster final of all time in 2004, and just under half the starting line-up were from west Waterford, which in itself was utterly unprecedented representation at that time. Those players inspired the senior players of 2024, and those west Waterford lads from 2024 were the players that our young players in An Sean Phobal looked up to.

The week before my first ever hurling training session, I had seen that Marc Ó Mathúna from Old Parish was on the Waterford under-20 team playing in the Munster championship. It's a sign of what's possible, even if you come from a club as small as An Sean Phobal. Waterford had a poor season at that grade, but Marc was one of their best players, and he can rightly have ambitions to make the next step.

As people were keen to tell me from the moment I moved down, numbers at hurling training were way up on previous football-only seasons, because it was so enjoyable. And the club were winning. Old Parish took three West Waterford titles in a row before they finally won the county Junior C title the autumn before I joined. The step up to Junior B was going to be challenging this year, but the team was confident, accustomed to winning, and had a spine from centre-back to full-forward that was for the most part young and full of running. And hurling was the preferred sport of every one of those lads.

Throughout the 1970s, '80s, and most of the '90s, Waterford hurling was nearly as low as Waterford football, but with hurling now definitively in the ascendancy, the Waterford County Board have acted accordingly. They were the only county in 2024 with a high-level club hurling championship that played their championships one after another, which is to say that the hurling championship was played off to a finish in mid-August before the football competition started the week after. Wexford had been doing likewise, but then decided to go with the overlapping championship format used by basically every other dual county, with hurling and football alternating every week or couple of weeks. The argument is clear: hurling is a summer sport, and should get the best of the weather . . . but it leaves football in no doubt as to which is the preferred sport in the county.

So this period, in mid-April and May, was the only time that we would really have to juggle our commitments between football and hurling. And this upcoming football game was what they might call in retail my 'soft launch'. I was given the number 14 jersey, and it was a relief to be able to show my new teammates that, contrary to what they'd seen heretofore, I am somewhat coordinated.

We lost the game to Dunhill 3–14 to 1–11, but I managed to kick a few scores, and my uncle was satisfied enough. Every point I contribute here, I said to myself, buys me one fresh-air shot at hurling training. A week later, we had another football league game, and we fell a few points short against Butlerstown. It was a bit of a culture shock to see how haphazard everyone's approach to the league was in Waterford, in both hurling and football – it was clear that the championship was the only show in town. I had been given a schedule of fixtures for hurling and football, but the exceptionally wet weather we'd seen in March and April had thrown that into utter disarray. There were games to be caught up from early in the season, there were rearranged fixtures, and the schedule was now worth about as little as the paper it was written on. It seemed to be everyone's view that these were games just to be fulfilled, by whichever players the club could lay its hands on. It didn't make a whole pile of difference to me, as I was just focused on feverishly trying to take on board as much hurling as I could handle.

But then the news came through in the huddle after the game: our next fixture would be a hurling league match, at home to Fenor, on the following Friday night.

We'd been training for football for the previous two weeks because of the football fixtures, so I hadn't had much chance to work on my hurling. And I was going to be in Dublin the Tuesday before the Fenor game for work, thereby missing the only team hurling session we'd have beforehand. This is where the rubber of my optimism would meet the cold hard tarmac of reality.

I expressed my concerns to Jamie Wall, and he suggested I spend the rest of the weekend studying the Munster hurling championship. Clare were playing Cork that weekend, and there isn't a more watchable player in the game right now than Clare's Shane O'Donnell. So what could I take from studying the best full-forward in the game, if, as I suspected, I was being groomed as a potential option for that position for whatever few minutes of hurling I'd see at some stage during the season? I could watch his close control, speed, balance, finishing power, and composure in slack-jawed admiration, absolutely . . . but as for teachable moments? Give me a break.

But Jamie had another idea. Why didn't I focus on his teammate Peter Duggan, who is about six foot four and has a catching hand the size of a ham. This might be a player for me to try to emulate. I was willing to accept there might be something in that for me, if I was willing to put aside the vast ocean of difference between his skill level and mine. His job on the Clare team is to play wing-forward, put said monstrous paw up for puck-outs time and time again, and to physically dominate opposition half-back lines. On this particular day, he was being marked by Cork's Tim O'Mahony, and what went on between the pair of them was nothing short of grievous bodily harm. Wild pulling, mid-air body-slams, and (I will introduce the term advisedly) outrageous flaking were par for the course. The welfare of various bodily extremities was treated in an extremely cavalier fashion. And this, apparently, was the role I was born to play. Was Jamie completely insane?

'Listen,' he said, 'the way I see it, if you go into full-forward, you might not have enough room to manoeuvre. You won't have the touch to get turned and facing goal, and you'll have a full-back looking to break ball off you using any means necessary. If you're out at twelve, maybe you can catch an odd one, get on a break, keep the ball moving forward. There's no major pressure on you to score, and there's no real tracking back required. I'm just saying it's a possibility.'

I watched Peter Duggan pick up his man-of-the-match award. He had a mark on his face like someone had attacked him with an industrial stapler. He gazed absent-mindedly at his melon-sized fist, double-checking with equanimity that he still had the full complement of fingers, as he waited for his trinket to be presented to him.

He looked like a Spartan, with his biceps straining against the sleeves of his jersey and his hair stuck to his head in a mess of sweat and blood. Peter Duggan is the dictionary definition of a warrior-athlete. Beads of perspiration started to gather at my collar. What the hell had I signed up for?

This feeling was not entirely new to me. The previous summer, I had been approached to play in goals for the Templeogue Synge Street senior footballers, owing to a chronic shortage of alternatives. I blithely accepted, blithely went through the motions for the few days beforehand. And then, with mere hours to go before throw-in, it hit me. I had volunteered to make an absolute show of myself.

That was how, with about fifteen minutes to go in a vital league game away from home, I found myself standing in front of the kicking tee, having lost three kick-outs in a row and thus thrown away a commanding position in the game. I desperately needed to find a receiver for one measly kick-out. In that moment, I swore to myself that I would never volunteer in so cavalier a fashion for something I was so intensely unprepared for. And yet here I was . . . sailing into a full summer of it.

I'd read George Plimpton (and even a bit of Paul Gallico, his predecessor), so I knew the genre of participatory journalism. This was a school of writing which held that you could not know a sport, and write knowledgeably about a sport, if you hadn't been in the arena yourself.

Whether that had been a motivation for going in goals that evening in Whitehall, I do not know – goalkeeping is a key role in Gaelic football now, and maybe I felt I'd be a better journalist and a better analyst if I'd experienced it even once (public humiliation be damned). But that suggests a deeper level of thinking about that incident than I remember giving it. In short, I wanted to help the club, and I was too dim-witted and proud to think that I'd be signing up for embarrassment.

My hurling adventure would be a slightly different kettle of fish.

For sports fans of a certain vintage, Plimpton is perhaps best-known as one of the talking heads in the *When We Were Kings* documentary about the 'Rumble in the Jungle', the world heavyweight championship bout between Muhammad Ali and George Foreman in Zaire (now the Democratic Republic of Congo) in 1974.

But he made his name long before that film's release twenty years later by embarking on a number of absurd assignments for *Sports Illustrated* and then later for the purpose of writing books. His first short book in this vein was *Out of My League*, which chronicled his attempt to pitch an inning to the best players in Major League Baseball.

He later wrote his most successful book, *Paper Lion*, about his time spent preparing to play quarterback for the Detroit Lions in an NFL pre-season game. When Plimpton – tall, patrician, the editor of the *Paris Review*, for Christ's sake – walked into the Lions locker-room and said he'd like to take four snaps under centre against another NFL team, it was a stunt, and everyone knew it. But the mere fact of my father's, my uncles', and my grandfather's involvement in the club made my situation very different from Plimpton's. I certainly couldn't approach my hurling summer as a stunt.

I found a PBS documentary about Plimpton's life, and some lines of his immediately resonated. He was 'the universal amateur', in his own words.

'The only way to understand the secret society is to become a member of that secret society yourself,' he says at one point. This is how I felt about every hurling conversation I ever took part in with a hurling person.

Plimpton, says one contributor to the documentary, was always 'looking for the perfect moment of total failure'. This would be far more easily achieved playing for Kilkenny in an exhibition game than it would be spending three months training and practising to play Junior B hurling in Waterford. By giving myself the slimmest of chances to succeed, I was making my life immeasurably harder. The less you knew about the game, the more likely you'd be inclined to think: How hard can it *really* be?

I knew better. The only saving grace, facing into my first ever game of competitive hurling, was that I would probably only be on the field for a mercifully brief cameo.

6

On Wednesday, Mam texted me to report that she and Dad were going to spend the weekend in Waterford. 'We haven't been down in ages,' she half-heartedly offered. But I knew the real reason. There was a chance I was going to make a fool of myself, and who wouldn't want to see that?

I told her that there was every chance that I wouldn't get any game-time. I also urged her to try not to make their arrival too conspicuous, in case Sean and the management saw them and thought they should throw me in as a charity case. She understood all that, but they were nevertheless intent on driving three and a half hours each way on the off-chance.

I called in to see them at my aunt Joan's house in An Rinn beforehand. I sensed a great feeling of anticipation in the kitchen as I walked in, a feeling I tried with all my heart to douse. Mam said, 'If I were you, I'd tell whatever fella you go in on tonight to stay well away from you, you're awkward and you're a danger.' She said this in all seriousness. It was both humiliating and, quite possibly, good advice. Maybe I had a moral responsibility to tell the man who was marking me that I'm liable to do anything, at any time?

I was taking my gear-bag out of the boot of my car at the pitch when Michael Hogan came up to me and told me that there was a chance I'd be starting. I was, quite frankly, appalled at this scenario. I still hadn't even trained with my teammates on a full-size field. I was glad of the heads-up, because it gave me time to try and focus on my achievable aims for the evening. Avoiding catastrophic injury was a major plank of my pre-game visualization. Apart from that, a few other thoughts were milling around.

The Tuesday beforehand, when I had been in Dublin for work, I had met my friend Sinéad O'Carroll before she drove to Celbridge for camogie training. On that occasion, I had tried to focus on the sort of skills that I thought might come in handy if I was going to get ten or fifteen minutes at the end of the game. If I could try and catch a few high balls delivered from fifty or sixty metres, that would probably be a worthwhile exercise.

I practised hand-passing, and after a few seconds of that Sinéad agreed that my best bet was to just throw it.

The hand-pass rule has been the subject of much discussion in recent years, as more and more teams moved to a style of play that prioritized keeping possession. This means more hand-passing, as Christy O'Connor documented in the *Cork Echo* around that time. In the 2017 and 2018 inter-county seasons, the average number of hand-passes per game was in the low seventies; a year later it had climbed into the mid-eighties. By April of 2024, the average had gone over 100.

A legal hand-pass is meant to feature two distinct movements – a 'release', and a 'striking action'. Under the rules, you aren't supposed to throw the ball. There's supposed to be separation between the hand and the ball before it is passed off.

In Gaelic football, which has an equivalent rule, you hold the ball in one hand and you fist or palm it away with the other. In hurling, you obviously can't do that without dropping your hurley, and dropping your hurley to hand-pass a ball is a foul. So the idea is that you have to release the ball from your hand before bumping it towards a teammate.

In inter-county hurling, this happens at such blinding speed, often in the middle of a ruck of players, that referees struggle to distinguish between legal transfers of possession and illegal throws. There was a sense that officials had given up and that all but the most obvious throws had become effectively legal.

Hand-passing is not quite as common at club level as at inter-county, but it's still a key skill of the game, and my attempts at legitimate hand-passing were so cumbersome, so unnatural, and so inaccurate that they tended to derail any move I might be involved in. If Limerick's Cian Lynch, the principal stylist in the game, could (rightly or wrongly) be accused of throwing the ball ten times a game, then I was probably as well off taking my chances with a throw or two.

After a few minutes of that, I stood in front of the goal, caught a few high balls that Sinéad sent in my direction and hammered them at the empty net, if for no other reason than to make myself feel good. I could have tried to practise twenty- or thirty-metre stick-passes, but realistically I didn't see myself doing a whole pile of that in my first match.

I was lifting the ball one-handed at the end of the session, which aggravated Sinéad even more than some of my other bad habits had done. 'What are you doing going at the ball one-handed? Two hands on the hurl.' She was channelling her own dad, and it was a terrifyingly effective pedagogic style.

I had never actually lifted the ball in anything other than the most benign of conditions – gloriously alone, a ball left on the ground, stationary, the only possible complication being that it might be covered in dog saliva. I saw no reason in that situation to approach the ball with any more than one hand on my hurley. But a game situation would be rather different. Instead of approaching the ball at walking pace, and nonchalantly sliding my bas underneath the ball and flicking it into my hand, lifting the ball in a game situation would have to be done as quickly as possible, with multiple other hurleys attempting to thwart me. Bending your back, with two hands on your hurley, gave you some leverage over the ball. Going in with one hand might have looked cool when Shane O'Donnell did it, taking him away from rucks like a bullet from a gun, but Shane O'Donnell I ain't.

Sinéad laid it on the line for me as succinctly as she could. 'Listen, you're probably going to get the ball into your hand three or four times max. The rest of the game will just be you mullocking about in rucks, using your arse as best you can to nudge people out of the way, and getting fouled. Lift the ball with two hands on your hurley, throw the ball to the nearest red shirt, and see what happens.'

On a balmy Tuesday night in Dublin, I had allowed myself to dream of loftier goals. Three days later in the pissing rain in Waterford, I was cursing Sinéad's optimism.

Our coach Tadhg came up to me before the game and confirmed that I would indeed be starting at fullforward. He told me to go out and enjoy it, that the league was just a place for teams to play a few games, find a bit of form, do a bit of experimentation. 'Just focus on the things that you're good at,' he said – before listing some things that I'm not terrible at in football. 'Stay close to goal, keep moving for passes, occupy the fullback. If a man is coming through the middle, get out of his way, give the full-back a choice to make. Get on the ball and lay it off to the man coming through. All very simple stuff, kid!'

Tadhg's leadership style is all about positivity – he's a naturally upbeat person who was hoping some of that might rub off on me. It was a valiant effort, but I had more primal things on my mind. What if my ankles don't survive? Should I say a tearful goodbye to them now?

The pitch was extremely heavy, and I struggled nervously through the warm-up, but in these conditions 'two hands on the hurley' was solid advice to fall back on. I saw my parents come in through the gate. I saw them peering at the number on my shirt as I ran back and forth from the end-line doing our warm-up. Did I hear laughter? No, of course not. That's not their style. They wouldn't disrespect me like that.

The game began. Almost immediately Fenor went out into an early lead. I was prowling around on the edge of the square, and to the untrained eye I might have passed for a hurler. I moved as if I knew what I was doing. And in many ways, as long as the ball was up the other end of the pitch, I did know what I was doing. I was staying deep, keeping the full-back honest. I was an option for the high ball . . . an extremely bad option, of course, but an option nevertheless. The fact remained that, my Croke Park dalliance aside, I'd literally never set foot on a grass pitch with the intention of hitting a sliotar in my life.

My first involvement came a few minutes into the game.

As play progressed down the left channel of our attack, I cut to my left and then back to my right, trying to lose my marker, in the traditional manner of a football full-forward. Here's a transferable skill – excellent! Bryan French put a lovely ball in front of me, along the ground. 'Two hands on the hurley, two hands on the hurley . . .'

But then, another option appeared before me. Another, sexier, riskier option. Our centre-forward, Conor French, had run past my left shoulder, heading for goal. Maybe if I could just pull on the ball, and put it out in front of him, he'd be through for a score . . . This required me to make contact with a moving ball, however, and I failed miserably to do that. The ball ran through my legs, and through the full-back's legs, and in anger I stormed into the ensuing ruck. I pulled, and immediately heard the dull thud of my hurley hitting the covering corner-back across the ankle. 'Fuck!' I said, out loud.

The corner-back didn't seem overly put out, and the referee hadn't seen it, so the corner-back simply drew his hurley back and whacked me across my knee. That appeared to be the ledger balanced. The ball was cleared, and nothing more was said about it. This double whammy of ineptitude (fumbled possession, followed by dirty stroke) would nevertheless prove to be my personal high point of the first half.

My height and size were a siren's call to my teammates, who sent a number of high deliveries my way. Some of them I went for with my hand. Others I approached tentatively in the air with my hurley. All were entirely outside my feeble powers to control. At one stage, a beautiful ball came in at head height from the left-half-forward position. I was moving out towards it and realized I'd never get a better chance to catch the ball and release it to a teammate. I dropped it, but it rebounded off my chest somehow to Conor, who put it over the bar from forty-five metres out.

This would count as an assist, technically speaking, but it was a ball I simply had to catch. It was massively frustrating. We were only two points down at half-time, but I felt completely deflated, and knew that I wouldn't be emerging for the second half.

As half-time wore on and no changes were announced, I realized they were leaving me on. This was incomprehensible, bordering on reckless. But I retook my position for the start of the second half and prepared myself for another few minutes of humiliation before they finally called me ashore.

John Flynn's brother Michael was hurling up a storm. He had done the majority of our scoring in the first half, and was in a good position again moments after the half began. He took a shot from about fifty metres out, and I watched it sail over my head on its way over the bar. But the ball tailed off as it got closer to the goal, and it hit the inside of the left post.

I was in close to goal for no other reason than the fact that I'd stood in that exact position a million times on the Gaelic football field. As the ball thudded off the post, the keeper lost his footing. The full-back was caught unawares, and in his haste to recover also fell down. I stared down at the ground, and there it was. The sliotar, lying in the muck at my feet, three metres in front of an open goal. 'What luck!' I thought to myself. And then I thought, 'Shit, I have to do something here.'

I pulled on the ball once to get it out in front of myself, and then pulled on it again as the goalie moved across goal in a doomed attempt to block it. The ball nestled in the back of the net, and I had myself a goal on my debut.

I have always really enjoyed scoring goals in Gaelic football. They're usually big moments in the game, and I know how I react in those situations. A clenched fist, or an exhortation to teammates, or a shoulder barge into the man I'm marking, if I'm feeling particularly pumped.

This was completely different. As I said to Sinéad when I called her the following day, I reacted in much the same way her two-year-old daughter Dani would do if she had performed some simple task that she had been asked to do. I wore the wide, gormless smile of a very small child . . . or an idiot, if you prefer.

I could hear frantic yahooing from the sidelines, which I could only presume was coming from my uncle

John. I couldn't understand a word of it, but Dad assured me afterwards that what John was saying was something along the lines of, 'It's just in his nature – it's the nature breaking out in him.'

I was so relieved to have scored, to have contributed something, but the goal also had the additional benefit of giving us a one-point advantage in the game. *This would be a perfect time for them to take me off* is not the mindset of a hardened competitor, but it was nevertheless exactly the thought I had as the ensuing puck-out was being taken.

The full-back had been happy enough to let me go up and try and catch the ball throughout the first half, secure in the knowledge that the only thing I was likely to do was take the pace out of it for him and let him pick it up at his ease and move it out of defence. But the goal might have stung his pride. The next ball that came in between us, I stuck my hand up to catch it. He pulled in the air to try and bat it down to the covering defenders he had in front of him. My hand was in the way, and the hurley caught me on the finger.

I reacted volcanically to this obvious red-card offence, before I realized that not alone was it not a sending-off offence, it wasn't even a foul. If I was foolish enough to put my hand up without sticking my hurley between my hand and where the defender would be pulling, I deserved whatever I got – up to and including a bloodied finger, and one that almost instantly started swelling up and throbbing with pain. I thought Sinéad's teaching style was forthright, but there is no better way to learn than getting your knuckle rearranged for you.

My troubles continued. I was still thinking about catching the ball, rather than simply catching it. I moved out onto another couple of balls, lifted a couple into my hand, and then just threw it out of my possession as if it were a bomb about to go off. I was exhibiting a complete lack of composure. Everything was going at a million miles an hour in my head, but at a sickeningly slow pace in real life. As Jamie Wall said to me on the phone the following day, 'Hurling is not a thinking man's game.' He's right: unless what you're doing is instinctual, it's pretty bloody hard to make any sort of an impact.

One ball that came to me was so perfect, such a pudding to catch, that I started thinking about the point I was going to hit before the sliotar was in my hand. In that instant, obviously, the ball was somehow dropped and the chance was gone. I had known that this was going to be difficult, but I really had no conception of how difficult it was going to be.

The nadir came with about five minutes to go. A ball went out for a 65, and I was the closest An Sean Phobal player to the ball after it had rolled out of play. So I went and retrieved it, tried to hit it back out the field to Michael, who was going to take it . . . only for it to skew off my hurley and very nearly behead the Fenor full-back, who was standing about ten metres in front of me.

I was left on for the full sixty minutes. This was a complete shock to me, and presumably to my teammates, to all fifteen people who were in attendance, and perhaps most of all to our opponents, who responded to my goal with a goal of their own and eased their way to a six-point win. But there was, in some weird way, a degree of sense in giving me the full game. If the league really wasn't the priority, then why not leave me out there? Training was great for developing the core skills, but there was nothing like a match situation to bring home how much work I had to do. As Sinéad had predicted a few days before, it was a bracing introduction to the practical application of the most basic skills imaginable. And Sean and Tadhg knew what everyone else on the panel could do. They didn't have a clue what *I* might be able to do. If the learning curve was steep, at least I had taken the first step along it.

When Tadhg said before the game to just do what I was good at, this must have been a reference to all of the lessons I'd learned in life and sport in the previous forty-one years, because it can't have been anything to do with hurling.

This, again, is maybe not quite as mad as it sounds. I knew how to move to the ball. If I could get proficient enough at the art of catching the ball and passing it to a teammate without having a panic attack, I should be able to pick out a runner and distribute the ball from full-forward, because I'd been playing that role for twenty-five years as a footballer.

For the moment, I could take comfort in one fact: I'd got a goal. Written down in the form of a text message to the dozen or so people who contacted me that night wondering how I'd gotten on, it was something to hang my hat on. I was a 'goal-a-game' man.

7

After another week of training, I decided to take advantage of my new southern posting and check out Cork vs Limerick in the Munster hurling championship at Páirc Uí Chaoimh.

Limerick were going in search of a fifth All-Ireland title in a row, something that no hurling team had ever achieved, and had begun their championship season with wins over Clare and Tipperary. Cork, meanwhile, had lost their first two games, and would have to beat both Limerick and Tipperary, and hope other results went their way, in order to progress to the All-Ireland championship. The Cork public had responded to the crisis in numbers, selling out the rebuilt Páirc Uí Chaoimh for the first time ever for a GAA fixture.

The Munster hurling championship might be the most reliably riveting ticket in Irish sport – and it has remained so despite significant changes to its format. Up until 1996, the Munster championship, like the All-Ireland championship, was a straight knock-out format, so eight months of training would come down to one day in the summer. That very last straight knock-out iteration saw the reigning Munster and All-Ireland champions Clare beaten in the last minute by a wonder-score from Limerick's Ciarán Carey, often acknowledged as the best winning point scored in the last seventy-five years of hurling.

The following year, the beaten Munster and Leinster finalists were allowed re-entry to the All-Ireland championship, and Clare and Tipperary played each other in both the Munster and All-Ireland finals, with Clare emerging victorious in both. If people thought that the creation of a back door to the All-Ireland would fatally weaken the importance of the Munster championship, they were mistaken.

Despite the fact the Munster championship routinely included five of the top six or seven teams in the country, it was still only four games in total every year – a quarter-final, two semi-finals, and a final. That changed in 2018, when a round-robin format was instituted. Each county played every other, with the top two qualifying for the Munster final and the team that finished third progressing to a preliminary quarter-final in the All-Ireland championship.

In 2020 and 2021, Covid forced a temporary reversion to a knock-out format, but the round-robin came back in 2022. Every year the round-robin has been played, the games have been almost unbearably good. And the various changes to the formats of the provincial and All-Ireland tournaments have never devalued the Munster championship: hurlers in the province desperately want to win it.

The secret formula that makes it so special for spectators is that every year at least one seriously good team, sometimes two seriously good teams, are eliminated. This level of jeopardy for high-quality teams is rarer in top-level sport than you'd think. Pool stages at soccer or rugby world cups are a way of easing big teams into the competition – they're seldom if ever about eliminating potential winners. The Munster hurling championship is beautiful in large part because it is so dangerous.

And that was what brought 45,000 people to Páirc Uí Chaoimh on a beautiful early summer day in Cork city, among whom were Jamie Wall and me. We were playing Cappoquin in our second league game the following morning, so I was going to drive back to Old Parish that night, but no one else seemed to have a care in the world. Jamie and a couple of his mates stopped in for a few pints on the way out to the Páirc, and the atmosphere was genuinely incredible around the city.

We got out onto the quays and walked the two kilometres or so to the stadium surrounded on all sides by young people occupying various points on the sobriety–drunkenness spectrum, families with kids, auld fellas with their jackets off and folded neatly over their forearms. It was a raucous body of humanity snaking its way out to the stadium, which looked utterly beautiful perched by the River Lee. If there was a better sporting event happening anywhere in the world at that moment, I'd like to have seen it.

If I was only embarking on my journey towards hurling respectability, Jamie's Hurling Man credentials were beyond reproach. He seemed to know pretty much everyone on the premium level, where he'd gotten us our tickets. I was helpfully holding Jamie's pint for him as our coach Tadhg walked past me, but I was able to offload it just in time to say hello.

'Are you ready for Cappoquin in the morning, boy?'

'I am, Tadhg.'

I really wasn't. But the fact I would be playing a game of hurling myself within about fifteen hours of the end of this one only added to my enjoyment of Cork vs Limerick. To say that I felt a kinship with Darragh Fitzgibbon or Patrick Horgan or Seamie Flanagan would obviously be ridiculous, but even just a few weeks in, I had a better understanding of how completely they must have dedicated themselves to this game for the fifteen years before they'd even started representing their county.

I always silently resented how hard our goalkeeper Dylan hit his short puck-outs whenever I was tasked with receiving one of them in the course of a drill or an end-of-session game. He seemed to absolutely hammer them at me (and at everyone else, too . . . but I cared less about those guys).

At inter-county level, the venom with which goalkeepers hit short puck-outs was on another plane altogether. The ball had to be delivered with enough pace that it wouldn't be intercepted by the exceptional athletes playing in the opponent's half-forward and full-forward lines. At almost every restart, the two corner-backs would stand on opposite sidelines, with their direct opponents standing about fifteen metres from them, trying to block up space to cut off the medium- and full-length puck-outs from the keeper.

This put enormous pressure on the corner-back's touch. Even the slightest juggle with the ball in their hand, or the tiniest hint of sloppiness with their touch off the hurley, and they would be swallowed whole with a tackle. The sharpness of their striking, the crispness of their touch, the sureness of their handling – I could see it with a different sort of appreciation now, and it was mind-bogglingly good to watch. Already I could see that one of the reasons why I was keen to play the game had borne fruit. I wanted an understanding of how difficult hurling was, and I was getting it.

The game was an absolute cracker. Cork launched a thrilling comeback in injury time to win by two. As I got into my car to head back to An Sean Phobal, I felt like the guy who was leaving Woodstock just as Jimi Hendrix was tuning his guitar. It was going to be a long, fun night, but I had Cappoquin to attend to in the morning.

I woke up at 6.30 a.m., and couldn't get back to sleep. I was feeling tired and a bit cranky when I stopped for coffee in Dungarvan on the way. I was sitting outside the café when the Second Captains superfan I'd met before my first training session pulled up outside. All he wanted to talk about was how brilliant the game the night before had been. As we were talking, three young men with glistening skin, impeccably groomed facial hair and powerful legs walked past us into the coffee shop.

'Those lads are Waterford hurlers, aren't they,' I said.

'Yes, yes they are,' the guy said. They were probably watching last night, too.

The coffee helped to put a bit of a pep in my step, and the drive out to Cappoquin was lovely. The GAA pitch is at the entrance to the village, and I pulled up just as the sun burst through the morning cloud cover.

If my first game was played in a monsoon, my second game was to be played in conditions that seemed, by the standards of early summer 2024, nearly tropical. The pitch was hard, and if it had a fair covering of sand, I felt oddly reassured by this: there would be much less digging around in the muck for the ball.

It was picture-perfect conditions for a game. And as I pucked around in the sunshine with the other early arrivals, in our shorts and runners, the thought occurred to me that this was summer hurling. True hurlers come into their own when the ground firms up and the sun comes out.

On closer inspection, the pitch was a little more rutted and uneven than I'd thought, but it was clear that if you couldn't hurl on a morning like this, you just couldn't hurl. I was not expecting to start again. But then the team-talk began, and management emphasized that we were still missing a few of our best players, out through injury and college commitments, and that now was the time for experimentation.

And so, when the team was named, I was once again at full-forward. I had been up and down to Dublin a bit that week, but had managed to make myself available for training, so I couldn't help but think that this was an acknowledgement of the effort I was putting in. No other reason for my being given a starting berth held water.

After our warm-up (more fumbles; striking at least decent; out-of-breath), we gathered for one last word, and then we jogged to our positions. My helmet felt tiny as the temperature crawled up towards twenty degrees. I was sweating rampantly underneath it. The full-back who came out to greet me was a lean man with a martial bearing who was almost as tall as me, broader than me across the shoulders, and about fifteen years younger. It promised to be a long day.

Cappoquin's first team played in the intermediate division. The lax eligibility rules for these league games meant that they appeared to be using this fixture to give game-time to at least two or three players from their first team who needed an early season tune-up. There were, in any case, a few lads playing a game that I was not even remotely familiar with. It may be stretching it to say that the man I was on was in that category, but I made him look like the hurling equivalent of Virgil van Dijk. The first ball that came between my man and me was overhit, and as I back-pedalled I was unceremoniously dumped on my arse and had to watch my marker pluck the ball out of the sky and sally up the field with it.

I'd spent most of the last game stationed very close to goal, but at training on Thursday night I had managed to string a few passes together from a little further out the field. I liked the idea of having a few touches, getting my head up and trying to pick out a pass, and so I tentatively ventured closer to the 45, trying to expand my horizons. We conceded two early goals, but we had brought the deficit down to a point (without any meaningful contribution from me) when I moved out to the left wing of our attack to try to find some space.

Patrick Conway, a veteran forward, had started the game really well, and he found himself in some room on the opposite wing. His cross-field ball to me was perfectly aimed and weighted; it hopped three times before it reached me; and yet it still beat my outstretched hurley by a full metre. This was directly in front of the sideline where most of the spectators were gathered, including, inevitably, my uncle, and it was just a humiliating moment.

Thereafter, my teammates were more circumspect about hitting the ball anywhere near me. I saw them look my way, ready to pass the ball to the man in a red shirt. I saw them realize who it was, maybe wince a little, and then look elsewhere for alternatives.

I know that look. On a football field, I've *given* that look. And now I was the recipient of it.

At one stage, our indefatigable midfielder Ciarán Ó Mathúna went on a solo run that saw him dispossessed twice, win the ball back twice, bounce the ball off the ground and finally hand-pass the ball to me after making a hundred of the hardest metres imaginable. When I got the ball into my hand, I had no better idea of what to do with it than to pass it straight back to Ciarán – and instead hit it straight to one of the three defenders who'd been hanging off him as he made his progress up the field. He slumped to the ground, and possibly shed a tear at the unfairness of it all.

At half-time, most of the talk from Sean revolved around making the ball stick in the full-forward line. For the others soldiering in there, I can presume there was an element of anger that it hadn't happened for them in that first half, maybe anger at being called out by

Sean over it, a refusal to allow it to happen again in the second half.

For me? I just felt complete helplessness. I had concentrated so hard on that ball from Patrick, and it beat my hurley by a metre. I was again given a chance to redeem myself, a chance I did not deserve. I went out in the second half and decided that the least I could do was sacrifice my body on the altar of something sore. There are plenty of ways to make yourself a nuisance on a hurling field, and some of them don't require any skill whatsoever.

A few minutes into the second half, a ball broke from our half-forward line and I raced into the corner with a man who was almost as slow as me. I didn't think I was going to get there in enough time to lift the ball, but I was damned if I was going to allow him to lift it. I saw him making the same calculation. I pulled from the hip and tried to whip the ball forward at the exact moment he did the same. His hurley hit my shin and calf with an oddly satisfying thwack. I was at least feeling something now that was not quiet despair or abject humiliation. It was a dull, reddening sensation rather than genuine pain, and I had left something on him too. I chalked it up as a win — even if the sliotar had flown out for a line-ball to Cappoquin.

I got one other ball put my way, which I lifted at the second attempt and then drove towards our best forward, Michael Flynn, on a cross-field trajectory.

The ball had at least travelled at the velocity and altitude I'd intended, but Michael was beaten to it by his opposite number. I was taken off soon after. My uncle ambled over to me once I'd taken a seat on the sideline. 'Jesus, boy, it's a powerful day, isn't it?'

'A great day for hurling, if you could fucking hurl.'

'Well . . . sure it didn't run your way.'

I wasn't going to leave it at that. 'You saw that ball in the first half. Sure Patrick couldn't have hit it more perfectly to me . . . and I wouldn't have stopped it with a catcher's mitt and a fucking tennis racquet.'

Silence is not a state one would readily associate with my uncle John, but this observation of mine rendered him temporarily mute.

We were six or seven down when I came off, but we hung around in the game, and a brilliant late goal by our wing-back Simon Lawrence had us within a puck of a ball with a couple of minutes left. There was even a half-chance from a late 65 to get a second goal and equalize, but we couldn't take it, and that was that.

I recounted my woes to Jamie on the drive home. ('I missed it by a fucking YARD.')

'Yeah . . . that sounds fairly depressing. It's bloody hard. OK, I think we need to get you some new hurleys.'

8

The hurley-maker Peter Flanagan in Tramore had been recommended to me by a number of people, but I couldn't get down to him before the first two games. So my two hurleys – one of which looked like it was near collapse, and the other of which looked like Baby's First Hurley – had to do in the meantime. The week of my first game, I had needed someone to replace the grip on the old one and duff up the new one, so that they might both look even a small bit like the sort of thing a hurler would actually use.

The deputy sports editor of the *Irish Times*, Pat Nugent, is from Tipperary, and this geographical fact alone meant he was just about the most qualified man I knew at short notice who I could ask to grip a hurley. He made no major claims for his abilities in this area, but I was back in Dublin for the day before my first game, and I was increasingly desperate.

I went up to the *Times* offices, hurleys in hand, and he inspected both of them with a gimlet eye. 'I'll replace the grip on this one', he said, holding my beloved old sword, 'but I wouldn't waste a grip on this piece of shite'. This was the sort of bracing insight I was looking for.

'What size is this thing, anyway?' he asked, pointing to the piece of shite.

It was a 33-inch hurley, I told him. 'I thought maybe I should experiment with the length of this shop-bought one, so that I'd have an idea what I actually want when I get a few made especially.' I sounded a lot more convinced of this logic than I actually was.

'Hmmm . . . Yeah, that makes sense.'

Yes! You're goddamn right it makes sense! I felt a growing affinity with the Hurling Man. The deliberate way Pat was grasping the grip suggested that this was a therapeutic experience for him. I asked him if he had any particular pearls of wisdom to impart.

'Peter is really well regarded. He'll be able to give you chapter and verse on what you need.'

'Well, yes . . . the only problem is I don't know what questions he'll ask me, and I certainly won't know the answers to them.'

Did I want a short hurley, or a long one? One with a big bas, one with a small bas? What are the pros doing these days? I heard that Galway's Cathal Mannion, one of the purest ball-strikers in the game, used a 32-inch hurley, which is very short for a man of his stature, well over six foot.

One way of measuring what length hurley you should have is to rest the stick against the side of your body: the top of it should stop just below your hip. By this principle, I should probably have a 36- or 37-inch hurley, not the 33 I'd bought a couple of weeks before. Pat had a newer version of this makeshift measuring scale. What you should actually do, by his telling, was hold the hurley with your arm hanging down by your side; the very bottom of the bas should just be grazing the ground. This method would more closely align a shorter hurley length with my chimp-like arms, and players now tend to use shorter hurleys than the hip-bone method would recommend.

Of course, length is not the only variable. There's also weight, as Pat was eager to tell me.

'Patrick Horgan has the heaviest hurley going. The size of the bas on his is a joke.'

Horgan is the top scorer in the history of the game, and this led Pat down a rhetorical byway, talking about how a broken hurley for your free-taker could in the past have meant the difference between a win and a loss, even in really big clubs. That's how attached hurlers get to their hurleys. Many purposely don't use the same one all the time, for fear of getting too fond of it and then potentially having to deal with it breaking at a key moment.

These days, fellas like Horgan can go to their hurley-maker at the start of the year and get six hurleys made to their exact specifications. The technology now exists for a hurley to be a more-or-less repeatable thing, even if a stick's 'balance' is a lot more difficult to quantify for the amateur than weight or length.

Players know what they like, and most of them stick with that. Other players enjoy tinkering with their style a little. I remembered hearing something about Shane O'Donnell, and a simple Google search brought me to an article, written by Maurice Brosnan in the *Irish Examiner*, the day after the 2023 All-Ireland semi-final that Clare lost to Kilkenny.

'O'Donnell has a PhD in Microbiology,' Brosnan wrote. 'His father, Martin, is a mechanical engineer. He makes the hurley that the Clare attacker uses. It is a uniquely manufactured stick, deliberated crafted to have no curvature on one side. Much like his magic goal, this complicated design is better observed than articulated.'

When we spoke on the podcast to Joe Canning around the time his autobiography was published, he talked to us about the hurley he'd made for the 2012 final, but he also talked about changing the length of his hurley at various stages, a quarter of an inch at a time.

Others are less concerned. Jamie Wall was Cian Lynch's coach at Fitzgibbon Cup level, and Lynch was so relaxed about his hurleys that he'd often show up without a spare. In the end, Jamie himself started packing one for Lynch . . . and gripped it too, as Lynch wasn't too bothered about a grip either, if whatever hurley he'd picked up happened not to have one on.

Pat's job on the grip of mine did the trick for the first couple of games. The following week, before we went to play Passage in our third league game, I made time to get to Peter Flanagan's shop in Tramore.

I wasn't in a position to ask Peter if I could choose the plank of ash from which he would make my perfect hurley. I just wanted to go into a shop full of perfectly made hurleys, hold a few of them in my hand, and then just go with whatever felt right to me. When I mentioned to Sinéad O'Carroll that I was going to Peter's shop, she got back to me a few minutes later with a request to get her a couple of hurleys too. No problem.

She then told me she was going to ask her sister, Suzy, one of Kildare's greatest ever camogie players, if she wanted in on the action. A couple of hours later, I got a screenshot of her order:

'Am I too late to ask Ciarán for a hurl? Size 34 – Tipp/Kilkenny style (previously West Waterford style) – anything around 500 grams. If he thinks I'm a lunatic and doesn't want to weigh hurls then that's fine . . . just don't get any if they're much heavier than that.'

Sinéad's reply was also visible:

'He's taken up hurling for the first time, aged forty-one. He is also a lunatic.'

Peter's workshop is in a different location from his

shop, so all I could see as I walked in the door were the fruits of his labour. On the small but perfectly appointed shop floor were various styles of hurley, arranged from smallest to largest.

There were hurleys in the Tipp/Kilkenny style, Cork/West Waterford, goalie's hurleys... I felt a little confused, but help was close at hand. I walked up to the counter and was greeted by a spectacularly upbeat and smiling woman: Peter's wife, Patrice. I told her that I'd like to buy a hurley but that I was not entirely sure what I wanted. I also mentioned that I also wanted hurleys for two other people. 'Eh, sorry, I'll just get the text message up in front of me here... it's for Suzy O'Carroll, in Kild—'

Patrice cut me off before I got to finish. 'Ah, Suzy... in Celbridge. She uses a 34-inch, right, and she likes them light? What else does the message say?'

This was the sort of boutique service I could get used to. Suzy's and Sinéad's orders were dealt with promptly, and then we got to my situation. At this stage, Peter had arrived on the scene. What sort of hurley would he recommend for a tall old man who doesn't know how to use one?

'Well, it depends ... do you prefer a big bas or a smaller bas?'

I looked at him imploringly. 'I suppose I want a big bas' – if only for the basic (possibly incorrect) physics of a larger bas making a fresh-air shot marginally less likely.

'Alright so, we'll get you a West Waterford one, and

shorter is OK since I don't think you'll be aiming to drive the ball a hundred metres. Does a 34-inch hurley sound good to you?'

I asked him what he thought about the relationship between your height and the length of your hurley.

'Well look at Limerick now, Sean Finn would use a 34-inch hurley. Longer than that, sometimes. I've seen him with a hurl and I'd swear it was a 35 or a 36 . . . I think he took an inch off this year now . . .'

This was all based on Peter watching at home on television, but I'd bet he was right.

'The height of him, he should probably be using a 32, given the way things have changed, with players generally wanting a shorter stick than the old method of leaning it up against your hip would say. But Finn shortens the grip all the time, and when he needs to hook or block, he'd just slide his hand from there' – a spot maybe four inches down the shaft of the hurley – 'back out to the handle, so he can use the full length of it defensively. Noelie Connors used to do the same thing, he used a 34-inch hurley as well. He'll be out in Passage tonight, you can ask him.'

I had heard a rumour that Noelie Connors, a three-time All-Star, might indeed be at this game tonight, and could in fact be lining out for the opposition. If he was playing, then he'd probably be playing full-back, and the thought of this was enough to make me break out in a cold sweat. Meanwhile, I still needed to have the idea of a hurley explained to me.

Peter was still talking, so I checked back in . . .

'So 36 used to be the length of an inter-county hurley, but that's changed now. It's 34 now, maybe less, and that's how the game has changed.'

Why was that?

'Short passing, playing through the lines. Players just want a hurley that's more manoeuvrable in those tight situations.'

So there were a couple of factors at play here. I'm six foot five, which would usually mean a 36-inch hurley at least. But I'm terrible at hurling, and a 36-inch hurley just seems unwieldy to me. I honestly feel like I'd be a danger with a hurley that long. If you're a sweet striker of the ball, then a 32-inch hurley is all you need. But again – I'm not a ball-striker. So 34 it is. Whether my logic holds up or not is almost secondary, because when I picked up a 34 from the rack, I liked the feel of it, and the weight of it – and that was that. I got two, to cover myself.

I was eager to know more about the different styles of hurley. And of course I was particularly interested to hear about West Waterford hurleys. Peter told me it had much to do with Justin McCarthy, the Cork hurling legend who came down to Waterford and led them to that first Munster final win in 2002. He encouraged his players to use a rounder bas, and in so doing changed what a Waterford hurley looked like.

I wondered what Austin Gleeson or Ken McGrath or

Michael 'Brick' Walsh said when they came into Peter's shop. If I was the type of hurler that knew nothing and wanted to be led by the nose, what did some of the best hurlers of this century say to him? As ever, that varied.

Ken McGrath and his brother Eoin often came out to the shop together during their long Waterford careers, and they were worlds apart. Ken would say he wanted a 36-inch hurley with a bit of weight, but after that it was – 'three hurleys, and you pick them out, Peter'. On the other hand, Eoin would want to see and feel half the shop.

Rather than sticking their oar in on the weight and feel of a hurley before the ash plank was even cut into pieces, it seemed most hurlers just wanted to hold as many hurleys as they could. And the feel of the hurley was decided entirely by the nature of the ash plank from which it had been hewn.

As the example of Ken McGrath demonstrated, not every inter-county player was pernickety about their hurley. Peter told me about another hurley-maker he had visited when he was still playing, before he started his own business. As was often the case at that time, he went looking to buy a couple of dozen hurleys for his club team, and then he said he wanted four for himself, and four for Patrice, who played camogie for Waterford. And he was told where he could choose from, but that there was a selection of the best that was being kept solely for inter-county hurlers. Peter vowed when he opened his shop that whoever walked in could get whatever they wanted.

Making hurleys for Patrice had nearly been the start of the entire trade for Peter, and of course camogie hurleys were different again; they were often much lighter, with a thinner handle. The fact that he caters for camogie players with absolutely the same level of care and detail as for hurlers is hardly notable now, but it certainly was when Peter started out. That generational difference is mirrored in his own kids, who idolize Beth Carton every bit as much as they do any male Waterford hurler.

Throughout this conversation, people drifted in and out, with Patrice dealing expertly with all their comments and queries. She was an adept shop presence, and the fact that she had been an inter-county player herself gave her instant gravitas. I got the impression after a while that people just liked to hang around and talk about hurleys. People feel good when they're talking about them, like musicians spending time in music shops even if they've no intention of buying anything.

It is one of life's genuine pleasures to talk to people who have forgotten more about one specific thing than 99 per cent of the populace will ever know.

Peter has thought deeply about hurley-making, about what it means for his own life, and he just wants to produce simple, beautiful objects that make people happy.

I didn't get a chance to see him crafting a hurley in his workshop, but he talked to me about how the one I was buying off him today would be something totally different in six or eight weeks' time, as the weather got better and warmer. Like a bottle of wine, like anything that was ever once alive, a hurley changes. Not alone is every hurley different to begin with: no hurley ever stays the same.

He talked to me as well about his own hurling career. When he was a youngfella, he was told to hold the hurley for as much of every day as he could get away with. He stopped playing ages ago, he says, but his touch was still good, because he had a hurley in his hand all day. He's so attuned to the weight and the feel of them that he can sense the sharpness of his touch in the wrists when he's knocking around with his kids.

Why did he give up playing?

'I couldn't do it and keep the business going,' he said. 'I got a couple of knocks on the hand, and I couldn't afford to pick up a knock. It wasn't just a business decision – honestly, making hurleys is too important for me. I love doing it.'

After I left him, I thought about that comment for half an hour or more. I couldn't make the link my brain was telling me was there. And then I remembered where I'd heard that line before. My friend Kieran Quinn, who won a Connacht senior football title as a midfielder for Sligo in 2007, told me the same thing about piano-playing.

He gave up Gaelic football because he couldn't afford a finger injury.

Whether it's playing jazz or making hurleys, it is a mode of expression as important to Kieran and Peter as anything they could do on a GAA field.

Artistry was, sadly, in short supply in Passage after I left Peter's.

It was midweek, so we were again short a few college players, and Marc Ó Mathúna had picked up a knock playing for the Waterford under-20s, so I started at full-forward again. The 'ignorance is bliss' confidence of day one, and the 'goal-a-game' run I found myself trying to maintain on day two, were both gone. What was left was a very poor hurler with very little confidence, and two very nice hurleys. My performance was basically an insult to Peter's hard work. The hurleys drew admiring glances in the dressing room beforehand – people walked across the room to pick them up and handle them, cooing appreciatively – but they were of little use by the time I got out on the field.

At least Noelie Connors didn't show up in his gear. He was there alright, looking a picture of health and charm on the sideline, but I was spared having to play against him. Other good news was hard to find. The view from the pitch across the Barrow estuary to County Wexford was nice, at least.

The story Sean told us after the game was that Passage had fielded four or five seniors who hadn't played much yet that season. Passage are actually the last Waterford club to win the county senior title before Ballygunner took over in 2014, and so I really hoped that was the truth, and not Sean trying to make us feel better about taking a bit of a hammering. As for my own performance – well, I recorded a voicenote on my phone on the road back to Old Parish, which began with a bracing summary:
I am shit, and I'm not getting better.
I just did NOT catch three balls that came into me.
I won a free, which Michael pointed.
I pulled on a ball in the air, which led indirectly to a point shortly after . . . or I moved it forward, at least.
I forced a fumble from their number 3, which led to a point. So that was good.
I didn't strike, catch or pass the ball. That's bad.
I was taken off at half-time.
And my hand hurts like crazy.

9

An Sean Phobal is a Gaeltacht club. So not only was I inflicting my utter lack of hurling pedigree on this blameless parish, I had also rocked up with an absolutely horrendous level of spoken Gaeilge.

Some people in my orbit in recent years have taken the view that my command of the language isn't actually that bad – this arising for the most part from my fearless willingness to trot out my terrible Irish, whether speaking to my best friend's two-year-old daughter Aoibh, who is being raised *trí Gaeilge* by her bilingual mum Sorcha, or by signing off various episodes of our podcasts with a few words, usually painstakingly checked in advance.

It's been interesting to experience the goodwill that this level of effort, which could charitably be described as the bare minimum, has received from native Irish speakers. But of course, one likes to be flattered and complimented, and so I have tried, with varying degrees of success, to get better at conversing plainly and normally in the first national language.

There were other factors at play, too. The success of the beautiful and devastating film *An Cailín Ciúin*, directed by Colm Bairéad and edited by my own brother John, was a huge catalyst. To have a sibling intimately involved in one of the key cultural milestones for the Irish language in the last fifty years couldn't but convince me to try to get my shit together.

Dad spoke Irish and English seamlessly in his childhood home, and so his Gaeilge was perfect. Or at least it sounded perfect to me as a child, on the odd occasion when he'd speak it in the house. But I think the status of Irish in the 1980s, when I was born, is very different from what it is now.

Gaelscoileanna are a far more integral part of the overall school pool now than they were even when I was a child. I think Dad would have seen the benefit of speaking more Irish in the home much more clearly if we'd all been born twenty-five or thirty years later – and we'd have been a much more receptive audience too, I feel sure.

There wasn't even TG4 until I was fourteen, by which stage I had no interest in practising my Irish with Dad: the culture of the time did not encourage me to do that. I think it's a very different landscape now for young people – and while the idea of my writing a book about their GAA club and their parish merited barely a shrug of the shoulders from my young teammates, the fact that I interviewed Móglaí Bap of Irish-language hip-hop group Kneecap that summer absolutely got their attention.

In any case, most of the time when I heard Dad speaking Irish, it was on GAA or governmental business. As part of his role as County Secretary, he would act as returning officer for Galway County Council, a job that fell easier to him than to many others, as he could move smoothly between Irish and English.

When Milltown were reaching county football finals in the 1980s, Raidió na Gaeltachta would have come looking for someone in the club with good enough Irish to go on-air to help them preview games, so Dad was a gift for them ... although my brother Paul remembers listening to Dad pre-recording RnaG interviews, and effing and blinding when he'd make a mistake. Getting that stuff right was important to him.

My brother John was no better or worse at Irish than I was in secondary school. But as an editor based at various times in his career in Galway city or just outside it, he got so much work with TG4 after he finished college that he really never had to do any supplementary courses – a couple of series' worth of *Paisean Faisean* episodes in his early twenties were enough grinds for any man. He's done three other feature films *trí Gaeilge* already, as well as the one that got all the way to the Oscars, so vast swathes of his working life are now experienced through Irish. It's something I'm really jealous of.

John never misses an opportunity to talk Irish to Dad these days, and Dad loves that. Mam did all her secondary school studies through Irish, and she and Dad happily speak Irish to each other in the house all the time now, particularly while they're watching the couple of games on TV every Sunday.

So for all kinds of reasons, I was determined to speak as much Irish as I could in An Sean Phobal. But . . . it's tiring. And when you're terrible at one thing (hurling, in my case), trying your hand at something else you're equally terrible at becomes even less appetizing a prospect. But hope was on the horizon, via the Comórtas Peile na Gaeltachta.

The Comórtas is a football tournament that brings together the best clubs from all the gaeltachtaí around the country – from Donegal, Kerry, Mayo, West Cork, and Connemara, from Rathcairn in Co. Meath, and of course from Gaeltacht na nDéise. Recent years have seen the inclusion of clubs in Belfast and Dublin, who compete and conduct their business exclusively through Irish. In counties like Donegal, Kerry, and Galway, there are multiple teams in both the senior and junior grades, and so they have county Comórtais, to decide who will represent them at the national Comórtas. But, in Waterford, An Rinn enter the senior Comórtas, and we're Waterford's only other Gaeltacht club, so we are the county representatives in the junior section.

Our record, it should be stated, was pretty modest at the Comórtas. In fact, we had yet to win a game at the previous editions we'd attended. But the Comórtas, to put it delicately, is not just a football tournament. It is also a beautiful celebration of Irish culture, a weekend of pride in one's *teanga, cultúr, agus caid* . . . and also, I was reliably informed, a monumental piss-up. Every story I heard from my new teammates or from my cousins in An Rinn about previous iterations of the Comórtas seemed to involve Olympian levels of drinking, debauchery, and, in some cases, minor public-order offences to which a blind eye was charitably turned.

I had barely been two weeks with the team when the message came through about the Comórtas: pay your €50, put your name down, and if we can muster a squad capable of competing, we're going. The 2024 edition was to be held in Cill na Martra in West Cork, and I was extremely pumped about the prospect.

While I was waiting for the June Bank Holiday to roll around, I read an essay by Brian Ó Conchubhair, 'The GAA and the Irish Language', in a book edited by Mike Cronin, William Murphy, and Paul Rouse called *The Gaelic Athletic Association, 1884–2009*, released to celebrate the 125th anniversary of the GAA's founding.

Ó Conchubhair's essay brought to my attention how closely linked the GAA was to the politics of the time. The co-founder of the GAA, Michael Cusack, was a native Irish speaker and an enthusiastic and engaged member of the Society for the Preservation of the Irish Language, the

Gaelic Union, and later the Gaelic League. Roy Foster's essay in the same collection shows how the GAA, the Gaelic League, and the Celtic Literary Society in unison formed a trinity responsible for a 'cultural revolution'. Foster quotes a passage from an 1892 lecture by the Gaelic League's founder Douglas Hyde, 'The Necessity for De-Anglicizing Ireland', in which he praised 'the brave and patriotic men who started the Gaelic Athletic Association'.

The Gaelic League and the GAA had quite a bit of overlap in membership, although Hyde regretted more than once, according to Ó Conchubhair, that the links weren't closer, even if both organizations collaborated in the 1930s on a magazine called *An Camán*.

There was an attempt in the early years of the GAA to penalize the use of English on the playing field, and although that didn't catch hold, the association's official guide in 2024 has on its very first page an assertion that 'the Association shall actively support the Irish language, traditional Irish dancing, music, song, and other aspects of Irish culture. It shall foster an awareness and love of the national ideals in the people of Ireland, and assist in promoting a community spirit through its clubs.'

Ó Conchubhair makes sure, too, to mention the one phrase of Irish that any Irish kid can immediately and joyfully repeat. Every GAA victory speech begins with 'Tá an-áthas orm an corn seo a ghlacadh . . .' and the speeches made exclusively *trí Gaeilge*, like those of Joe Connolly in 1980 or Sean Óg Ó hAilpín in 2005, are the ones that stand out most readily in the minds of GAA fans.

For young GAA players in the 1980s, the ambition was to play for your county minor team in an All-Ireland semi-final or final, which at that time were among the very few games to be shown live on RTÉ television every summer. Those minor games were always broadcast in Irish, and so that dream was always seen and heard and visualized in Irish – whether that was Micheál Ó Sé pointing out some vague familial connection of yours to a former great, or simply a recitation of your club name *as Gaeilge*.

Most of the Irish I would have heard in any given week in my Dublin life was via TG4's coverage of GAA games. The commentators do a wonderful job of catering to everyone, regardless of their level of competence at Irish. Their team of analysts combines native Irish speakers, national-school teachers (with their specific brand of grammatically correct, easy-to-understand Irish), and enthusiastic amateurs, in which group I would without a moment's hesitation include two good friends of mine, the aforementioned Jamie Wall and Paul Rouse.

They would both admit that their grammar is not perfect and that they would not have the blas of a native Irish speaker. But they barrel on, they absolutely make themselves understood, and their love of the language shines through. If people like me are to be engaged by

Gaeilge, then it will be people like them doing most of the heavy lifting.

It must be acknowledged that there's a limit to how much the GAA can achieve in promoting the Irish language, given that it is still after all primarily a sporting organization. But its ubiquitous presence on TG4 twelve months a year does a number of things. It keeps Irish fresh in the minds of casual GAA fans, it connects the language with a sense of fun and enjoyment and occasional ecstasy, and it also provides a platform for so many young players fresh out of Gaelscoileanna to showcase their Irish, and to normalize the idea of young people absolutely conversant in the language. I'm thinking in particular of one moment at the start of the 2024 national football league, when Dublin's Con O'Callaghan accepted a Laoch na hImeartha award after a game on TG4 and then did his post-match interview in faultless, relaxed Gaeilge.

The reaction on social media was predictable: 'He's an exceptional hurler and footballer, he's good-looking, AND he speaks Irish – is there anything this guy can't do?' Connecting the language to someone like Con is absolutely priceless, and that nexus of the GAA and TG4 allows it to happen.

In any case, during those early weeks in An Sean Phobal I was doing my best – never suspecting for a moment that I too would soon be prevailed upon to aid in the promotion of our native language.

*

Once we had informed the Comórtas organizing committee that we had a panel of over twenty souls available to head to Cill na Martra for the weekend, we were invited to send an emissary to the media launch of the competition, in Croke Park in mid-May. Sean had heard my conversational, basic Gaeilge during training, and suggested that I do the media launch, given I could very easily arrange my working week so that I would be in Dublin on the appointed date.

Now, as a regular punter, I would have immediately told Sean to piss off at his earliest convenience. But as a content creator, I knew this was not an invitation I could turn down. I said yes without a second thought.

I turned up to the launch in my brand-new An Sean Phobal jersey, having borrowed the number 14 at training the previous night. A lad from Carna-Caiseal in Connemara turned to me and told me *as Gaeilge* that I looked the absolute image of that lad Murph, from Second Captains. 'Is Murph mé . . . eh, tá mé, eh . . . Murph. Murph is ainm dom.' How I ended up at the Comórtas took a degree of explaining, but I got there.

I was only capable of explaining my situation to my Connemara interlocutor because I had spent the previous night putting together my Comórtas stump speech. My blithe optimism lasted until the evening before, when I suddenly realized that I wasn't just going to be able to style this one out. Every club had sent a representative because it was important that they make a statement that theirs was a club where Irish was cherished, and a central part of their way of life. This wasn't one of those situations where personal humiliation would be the sum total of how bad it could get. I really was a representative of An Sean Phobal, and I mustn't actually mess this up too grievously.

There was only one way to get through it. Regardless of what questions I was going to be asked by TG4, I would give them my stump speech. I had written out in Irish what I wanted to say, with some input from Jamie. I didn't want to go Google-translating every line. For a start, if I tried learning off a speech by heart that I had just Google-translated directly from the English, I felt sure I'd miss a word or two here or there, and it would be utter gibberish.

I thought it was better to just write the Irish that came to me, that I felt reasonably sure would sound at least vaguely comprehensible, and that I could speak without feeling like too much of a fraud. I also took a punt on what kind of interview it would be. The way I saw it, if TG4 was sending a reporter to a gig like this, it would be for a three-minute edited piece for their nightly news show, with each club who sent a representative featuring for no more than a few seconds. If it was a sit-down interview, with a back-and-forth required to make it work for the reporter in question, I was obviously screwed. But if I could talk my way into the reporter's good books, tell them what I had and what they could use, I might just get away with it.

I stood for photographs, I posed with trophies, all

the time waiting for my moment of truth. What really deflated me was my inability to maintain a conversation with my fellow players for longer than twenty seconds without interminable pauses, excruciating seconds while I searched in vain for the *cúpla focail* required to get to the end of a sentence.

In the end, the TG4 reporter couldn't have been sounder. I tried to explain to him in Irish my reticence to sit for a formal interview, and he just told me to deliver what I wanted to say, and he'd find something usable. So I sat down, with my phone out in front of me in case I got really stuck, and gave him what I had.

> Rugadh mé i nGaillimh, ach is fear An Sean Phobal é m'athair. Is craoltóir agus scríbhneoir mé, bím ag obair ar phodchraoladh Second Captains, agus scríobhaim colún leis an *Irish Times*.

(Some biographical detail to begin with, in case my interlocutor was a fan of the podcast and was wondering what the hell I was doing in Waterford.)

> Tá mé ag scriobh an dara leabhar faoi cursai Cumann Luthchleas Gael anois, agus cupla mí o shin, rinne me an chinne go bhfeadh mé nios sásta e sin a dheanamh sios i nGaeltacht na Déise, i measc mo chol ceathracha, so tá me ag imirt peil, ag imirt iomanaoicht, agus ag iarraidh mo chuid Gaeilge a fheabhsú sa Sean Phobal.

Tá me I dtriobloid leis an Gaelinn, ach tá mé i nios mo dtriobloid leis an iomanaoicht, más feidir leat é sin a chreidiúint.

(A quick summary of my current work–life balance, with a self-deprecating little gag about how terrible my Irish, and my hurling, are.)

Is brea liom an teanga, ba mhaith liom Gaeilge níos fearr a labhairt . . . gaeilgeoir is ea m'athair, bhí mo dearthair John ag obair mar eagarthoir ar *An Cailín Ciúin* . . . mar sin, níl aon leithsceal agam!! Ach tá mé an-brodiúil bheath ag imirt le chlub mo shinsir – is mothúchán an-speisialta é.

(I may not be a *gaeilgeoir*, but I know numerous *gaeilgeoirí*, so that has to count for something, right?)

D'imir me peil le Gaillimh fé fiche haon fadó fadó, ach ní raibh mé sa chomórtas riamh, tá mé ag súil go mór leis.

(Some pointless bragging about football from a previous century, basically, just to further endear myself to my audience.)

Bhí an Sean Phobal ag glacadh pairt don Chomórtas le deich bhlian nó mar sin, ach beidh muid ag lorg an chead bua an bhliain seo i gCill na Martra.
Bhí droch-ádh orainn leis an tarraingt sna blianta roimhe

seo, d'imir muid go leor de na buaiteoirí deiridh sa chéad bhabhta.

An bhliain seo, beidh muid ag imirt Na Gaeil Óga on mBaile Atha Cliath sa chead babhta, so bhí droch-ádh orainn arís, ach tá an foireann go leir ag tnúth go mór leis an gcluiche.

(A quick history lesson, and then some mind games to throw the hacks off the scent of our impending ambush . . .)

Is deireadh seachtaine stairiuil é, so mar sin ta mé ag tnuth go mór pairt a glacadh.

(. . . before I stick the landing with some pointless boilerplate.)

That's what I had on my phone, and that's what I ended up giving him, more or less — so any errors repeated here were errors I made on the day. I tried my best to remember it all, but I had my phone held just out of shot, so any on-screen moments where it looked like I was gathering my thoughts while staring off into the middle distance were actually just moments where I was trying to find the line I was looking for in my phone notes. I reckoned I had just about gotten away with it, and the message was at least delivered.

The script I had written out contained a couple of words I wasn't familiar with, words I'd had to look up, including how to say 'forefathers', or 'ancestors', *as Gaeilge* – *mo shinsir*, which I love. *Sinsir* is the word used in GAA circles for 'senior', as in your first team in adult football would be your *foireann sinsir*. But it evoked in me this image of my long-dead grandfather, who passed on my father's twenty-sixth birthday in 1974, or my beloved Nana, who died in 2004, all my relatives born and raised and now buried in An Sean Phobal, not as names on a family tree but as 'seniors' that I could lean on for advice and counsel. I don't think I'll ever be much good at Irish, but I was glad of the opportunity to use that word, at least.

The interview wasn't released until the week before the Comórtas and, as expected, they broadcast only a few seconds of it, but out it went on the TG4 news . . . and it wasn't actually that bad. I walked out of Croke Park that day absolutely exhausted from the effort, but ready for the Comórtas . . . *réidh chun dul*.

I set off from Old Parish on the Saturday morning, half expecting to be travelling in convoy with some of my teammates. But it turned out quite a few of them had been down since the night before, sampling the atmosphere, attempting to carb-load and getting settled in their accommodation. Whether some of them had done what Comórtas teams often do – have a few pints – I chose not to find out, but I had my suspicions.

We had been drawn against Na Gaeil Óga, the team

from Dublin, based in the Phoenix Park and made up entirely of *gaeilgeoirí*. I had played against them a number of times for Templeogue Synge Street in the previous three or four seasons, and I knew they were pretty decent, and that the Comórtas would be a big deal for them as a club. I also knew that in comparison to playing other teams from other counties, like Donegal or Kerry or Galway, this might be a decent chance for us to break our Comórtas duck. Convincing my teammates of that seemed to be a struggle, however. They saw Dublin, and they presumed we were in trouble.

I was far from sure how the Dublin side had been moving in the early part of that season, but in the huddle beforehand I described them as 'a fucking drinking circle' and 'a way for young lads to meet women'. This was an utter lie and a calumny. I'd spent the entire press launch having a great chat with their men's and women's representatives, who were so patient with my terrible Irish, and whose passion for the language and for Gaelic games in an urban setting was an inspiration – and this was how I repaid them! But I was trying to make a point about why we should be expecting to beat them . . . a point undermined somewhat by at least three of my teammates saying it sounded familiar and/or like a pretty good deal.

In the end, we played brilliantly. We were full value for our win, and it was genuinely such a pleasure to play in an atmosphere like the Comórtas – an immaculately appointed ground, a feeling totally unlike playing a club game in your native county. And the entire build-up, the discussion between the players and the referee ... all *as Gaeilge*.

I couldn't wait to get back into the car and ring Dad. He'd been following it via the An Sean Phobal WhatsApp group, and via Raidió na Gaeltachta, so he was well apprised. The second-to-last time the Comórtas had been on in Galway, he'd been out in Maigh Cuilinn with Mam watching An Sean Phobal, and he knew what a massive deal it was for the club. He would've loved to be there, I knew that. For all that he was supportive, or at least amused, by the idea of my playing hurling for the club of his birth, he also really wanted me to make some kind of mark with the football team. Whatever happened in the rest of the year, winning a game on a national stage like the Comórtas was a big deal.

We both tried to express that *as Gaeilge* at first, and then in English, without much success either way. But it was special. I was staying in the home of two Cill na Martra GAA members: Nollaig Ó Laoire, who just happened to be one of Cork's all-time footballing cult heroes, and his wife Eimear. They were both also playing in the Comórtas for Cill na Martra as well.

Our first ever win in the Comórtas was something worth celebrating, but there was the small matter of a *cluiche leath-cheannais* the following morning. It soon became clear that we would be playing Lispole, from Kerry. We were left with a decision to make. Could the seventeenth best team in Kerry be beaten by the twenty-fourth-ish best team in Waterford? We looked deep into our own souls, and decided that, on balance, no, that probably wasn't going to happen, so let's have a few pints and let the semi-final take its course.

We were drinking in Tigh Ó Murchú in Cill na Martra that evening, when I had slight pangs of guilt that I wasn't watching the Champions League final (given I was technically still a co-host on a sports podcast, and hadn't entirely left my normal life behind me). On one screen was TG4's YouTube channel, showing the latest game from the Comórtas, which was happening across the road. On the other screen was the All-Ireland under-20 hurling final between Offaly and Tipperary in Nowlan Park, also broadcast by TG4. It didn't seem like the sort of crowd in which to start kicking up a fuss over Real Madrid, so I settled in for an evening of our native games, in our native language. It was beautiful. Making myself understood in the general run of conversation was a challenge, but it was great fun nevertheless. And, as I knew it would, it brought me so much closer to my teammates. It set me up for the summer, to be truthful.

The following morning went pretty much as expected. We fell into a daunting early deficit, and the gap never really looked like being closed. Thankfully Lispole were sufficiently good to ensure that we were under no illusions – we'd have been well beaten even if we'd gone to bed straight after we'd had our dinner the evening before.

Later that week a report from the Comórtas, written by a devotee of our podcast, was published in the *Tuairisc* newspaper, and it was instructive indeed to learn that being called old and slow in a different language was as much fun to read as it would have been in English. This would be the last game of football we'd play for almost three months. From here on out, it was hurling all the way.

10

For six weeks of the summer, Gill and I stayed in a cottage in a place called Kilgobinet, halfway up a mountain in the Comeraghs and four miles from any public amenity . . . apart from a handball alley no more than a hundred metres from our front door.

This was quite frankly an extraordinary stroke of luck, and I did not take it for granted. Part of what makes hurling so hard is that it requires the execution of skills at extremely high pace, and there is almost always at least one opponent nearby with the capacity to thwart you. But it is possible to hone one's skills entirely alone – and there is no better place to do so than a handball alley, a crucible in which a hurler can be formed.

Of course, many hurlers didn't grow up with a ball alley so near, and had to make do with the gable end of their own house, or shed. It was good enough for plenty of the best hurlers of the last century. But this involves the constant danger of broken windows, and interruptions from livestock, or pets, or parents looking for jobs to be done. The pebbledash of the typical Irish home also rips sliotars to shreds even more quickly than my dog does. But I had no such worries in the handball alley at Kilnafrehan East.

As a Gaelic footballer, there is nothing I love more than practising free-kicks. It's a chance to focus on the simple act of making contact with the ball in the way that you want – a solid, repeatable action that you can depend upon in moments of stress. Kicking a ball is a completely unconscious act to me. You could not, under any circumstances, say that about my hurling stroke, and so every free half-hour I had, I was down to the ball alley.

The Kilnafrehan ball alley has been in existence for almost 200 years, as the little sign beside it tells me. It appears on the 1841 Ordnance Survey map, as I know because when I went looking for a bit of history on it (200 years seemed like a hell of a boast, even when my landlord Paddy insisted on it), I found an entire website dedicated to the history of Irish handball alleys. Much of the heavy lifting had been done by a Berlin-based Irish architect called Áine Ryan, who had no interest in the sport but a lot of interest in the structures themselves and what they might tell us about life in Ireland in the nineteenth and early twentieth centuries in particular.

Happily disappearing down an internet rabbit-hole, I was intrigued to see the *New York Times Magazine* covering the gradual desertion of local handball alleys across

Ireland, along with a hundred or so words on the history of the sport, all of which were useful to me:

> A century ago, handball was one of the most beloved sports in Ireland, its typical three-walled alley, or court, a fixture in villages and at crossroads. But these were 'more than just places where people came to play handball', says the photographer Kenneth O'Halloran, who visited nearly a hundred abandoned courts in Ireland and Northern Ireland last year. 'People came to socialize, to dance.' After the game moved indoors around the 1950s, many courts that were not demolished became places for parking or storage.
>
> There is little nostalgia among the Irish for handball alleys, O'Halloran says. 'I don't think people would value them the way they value a traditional cottage, old crosses or ancient ruins,' he says. 'A lot of people see them as eyesores.'

This is certainly true. But they are a reminder of a time, throughout the nineteenth and twentieth centuries, when handball was very popular across Ireland. It was the most frequently mentioned recreational activity in a School Inspectorate report from 1910, and the Irish Handball Council, a GAA subsidiary, formalized the game's competition structures in 1924, ahead of the first Tailteann Games (a sort of Gaelic equivalent of the Olympics).

The big handball names of the 1920s and 1930s were well known and featured in sports-card series. Match reports, new construction plans and court openings all featured regularly in the national newspapers. The game was played all over the country. Its popularity extended into my father's time – he remembers playing handball constantly in his youth, and he also remembers being heavily beaten, as everyone was, by one middle-aged gentleman from Old Parish who could barely move across the court but was incredibly skilful. In the 1950s, handball organizations made the perfectly reasonable decision to take the game indoors, removing the vagaries of Irish weather from the equation. But that decision also robbed the game of its social element. Outdoor handball alleys were a place for people to meet, to exchange gossip and news, and to hang around when there was little else to be doing with your leisure time. Indoor courts, for all their advantages in a sporting sense, were not capable of recreating that sociability. The game's dramatic drop in popularity over the decades that followed presumably had something to do with that.

The game is still played in pockets around the country, and is experiencing a mini-revival at the moment, powered in no small part by extensive live coverage on TG4. There are plenty of recent and current inter-county hurlers who were also exceptional handballers in their youth – Richie Hogan is perhaps the most famous, and Mikey Butler, his erstwhile teammate with Kilkenny, as well as Clare's Mark Rodgers, Adam Hogan, Peter Duggan, and David McInerney all played the game.

The *New York Times* article carried with it a gallery of twenty photos, taken by O'Halloran, and there it was – the Kilnafrehan East handball alley. Since those photos were taken, the alley had been restored somewhat, with the help of some state funding. The graffiti on the wall ('Kilgobinet Boys' – Kilgobinet being the local GAA club – along with something about Spurs, and a hastily scrawled MUFC, among other things), had been cleared, the wall on the left-hand side of the court rebuilt entirely, and the wall on the right renovated for about half the length of the court (the other half left open to the elements), and an entrance built by the side of the road. An overgrown bank for supporters at the back of the court had been stabilized and cleaned up to some extent.

The alley itself, situated at the junction of two roads, is a 60 by 30-foot court. The wall off which you played the ball is thirty feet high, the old GAA standard size. The hedgerows on either side of the road that runs downhill stopped quite a few balls that I couldn't handle over the course of the summer.

The open back end of the ball alley in Kilnafrehan offers a beautiful view down the mountain, and out to Helvick Head, where An Rinn looks out across at Ballinacourty, Abbeyside, and then west to Dungarvan, at the mouth of the bay. That's what I could see as I recovered the balls that had beaten my hurley, the balls that were struck so poorly that they rebounded nowhere near the spot where I was waiting.

If there is some recognized system to training in a ball alley, I have no idea what it is . . . other than just hitting as many balls as you can. The further back you stand, the more you can work on trying to add length and power to your stroke. This feels good . . . but then again, I lost two or three sliotars over the top of the wall and into a field of thistles directly behind. In addition, there was an element of unearned vanity to this. Nothing I'd done in any of the games I'd played so far suggested that I'd be hitting seventy-metre passes or shots. Nothing would give me greater pleasure than to *oscail do ghualainn*, as they might say on TG4 – 'open the shoulders' – and hurl all before me; but Brian Lohan or Tony Keady I am not.

What I needed to work on, desperately, was my first touch, and my catching. If I could manage to improve either or both of those, then that would be a gateway into the sport. Everything flowed from those two skills, and everything ground completely to a halt in the absence of either. So Gill would head off every morning for a swim in An Rinn with my cousin Bríd, or at nearby Clonea Strand, and meanwhile I'd walk into the alley, stand myself about five metres from the wall, and beat sliotars off it for twenty minutes at a time.

Here's how it generally went. The balls I drove low at the wall came back to me low, and I stuck my hurley down to try to corral the ball into my possession. The concrete floor in the alley gives you a far more regular bounce than you get on a grass pitch, but the basic skill involved is transferable. I tried firing it at my feet time and time again, and after a while it started to come. Whereas at my first training session, the ball would bounce off the bas of the hurl I held in my left hand and fly about nine feet in the air over my right shoulder, I had by this point managed to bring that down to about six feet. It was still unruly, but if I could react quickly enough, I might be able to catch it before it reached my right ear.

This was progress.

A problem had developed elsewhere, however. The ball along the ground will always be controlled by the hurley. But anything above shin height you should be going for with your hand. And my hand, my right hand, my catching hand, was taking a terrible beating.

I was not unfamiliar with this feeling. I've already mentioned how sore my hand was after spending a couple of hours playing D-O-N-K-E-Y with friends in the Phoenix Park a few years ago. We were messaging each other for days afterwards, wondering if we should go to the hospital for an X-ray.

When I started training, that dull pain came back, and I just shrugged it off. I presumed I'd develop some kind of hurling callus, and I'd get used to it. But the pain really, really wasn't going away. And it was hindering my progress in these ball-wall sessions.

When the pain started getting worse in the ball alley, I'd

stop, as I've done in all life situations where I[...]
avoidable. But down at training was a differe[nt...]
I didn't feel I could just stop in the middle of [a]
session and say, 'Listen, my hand feels like it's abo[ut to fall]
off. I'm just going to step away for a few minutes here.' I
couldn't do it, even though I really wanted to.

I decided I would get myself a glove for my catching
hand. This was not exactly a galaxy-brained idea. When I
got that initial blast across the knuckles from my direct
opponent, I thought it would be the first of many. But
now I knew that the real issue wasn't protection from
other hurls: I needed protection from the bloody sliotar.

In Waterford city I went around a couple of the sports
stores before I found a glove that I thought might fit me.
I got it, tried it on, paid for it . . . and then threw it in
my bag and didn't wear it. I was ashamed of it. I don't
know why. T. J. Reid, possibly the greatest hurler of all
time, wears a glove. So does Richie Hogan, another Player
of the Year. Dozens of inter-county hurlers wear a glove.
My nephew Enda has always worn one. But I was being
an idiot. And my being an idiot extended even to the
ball alley.

I was afraid that the neighbours would see me with the
glove on. The fella who lived nearest the ball-wall used
to shear my uncle John's sheep, and I didn't want him to
think I was soft. My landlord for the summer thought
my uncle John to be the greatest character in all of west

Waterford, and I didn't want him to think the bloodline had been reduced to this – a glove, just to go hit a few balls against a shaggin' gable.

I was also afraid that the local national-school kids, who got on and hopped off the bus at the junction where the ball alley was situated, would see me with it on. Often I'd have to move their beautiful expensive new bikes, which they'd leave unlocked inside the alley against the ball-wall in the morning. I was being bullied by a retired farmer, a sheep farmer, and their bike-owning grandkids – and none of them knew anything about it.

The terrible state of my hand was obvious to anyone who looked at it for even a moment. The area from the lower knuckle of my middle and index fingers to the centre of my palm was, at various stages throughout May and June, purple, bright blue, yellow, and brown. It was genuinely disgusting.

There was little or no pride in my showing off my hand, because even before I'd started hurling, I had a couple of fairly deformed fingers (the little finger on both hands), having dislocated them while trying to catch footballs. My ring finger on each hand is also a little bent out of shape.

But these deformities are as nothing compared to the hands of most hurlers. The *Irish Examiner* had a series called 'Hurling Hands', in which they'd talk to a former hurler about the state of their digits. The accompanying photos ranged along the spectrum from 'gnarly' to 'do these belong to a human?'

All the interviews followed vaguely the same pattern, whereby the person being interviewed would say that they had got away quite lightly in comparison to some of their teammates . . . before outlining that they'd suffered multiple broken fingers, broken thumbs, exploded nails, smashed forearms. If this was lucky, then unlucky doesn't bear thinking about.

I've had the great honour of meeting and chatting with the Tipperary hurling legend Nicky English on many occasions over the years, and the man's hands are intimidatingly misshapen. His handshake is indicative of someone whose nerve-endings were shredded many moons ago. He grabs your hand and squeezes it like you'd squeeze a lemon, to the accompanying sound of your ligaments tearing and your bones breaking.

In any case, I knew I was catching the ball incorrectly. It's supposed to roll from the tips of your fingers down, not come charging like a bullet into the upper half of your palm. Fingers are more supple, can bend and move and cushion. They can spread the impact across themselves. I looked it up, and it seemed that the middle and ring metacarpals were the bones I was in most danger of breaking. But it wasn't just bone – it was the tissues around those bones that were constantly turning purple and yellow.

The pain was affecting both my enjoyment of training

and the progression of my skills. I used softer balls in the ball alley from time to time. But I was down there to practise for game-specific circumstances, and I knew that meant I ought to be using sliotars. Each training session I would jog out onto the field, eager to see if there was something I had improved since the last session, and I would be generally upbeat before the warm-up began.

And then that first ball would fizz in my direction, and the pain would explode through my hand and up my arm. I'd get home, put my hand in a bucket of ice, and convince myself that there was nothing to be done but wait for the hoped-for hurling callus to develop.

What really hobbled me was that at one stage relatively early in the piece, I had asked Patrick Conway, a man of roughly my vintage, if he ever got pain in his catching hand. 'Oh yeah,' he replied. 'For the first two or three weeks every spring, it would be sore, but then it pretty much goes away.'

This was what I was clinging on to. I wanted to just get through this rough period, and then be able to catch without the use of the glove. Bearing Patrick's words in mind, I kept thinking to myself that I should stay patient, and I'd be alright. But the truth was that doing without the glove was just stupidity. The pain should've made my mind up for me after a week.

The ball alley helped me get comfortable swinging my

hurley to make contact with the ball 99 per cent of the time, helped to build up my wrist strength (which in turn allowed me to shorten my swing and avoid getting hooked), and it helped to get my hand used to catching the sliotar. The hours I spent there definitely made a difference.

But the alley was still a pale imitation of the real thing.

11

One of the key attractions of hurling, to the outside observer, is the feeling that you are watching people who have absolutely no regard for their own personal safety. This was, of course, even more true in the days when players didn't wear helmets. Loose hurleys used to be able to do terrible damage to players' heads – a back-swing or a follow-through sometimes found a forehead or a cheekbone or, even more devastatingly, an eye-socket.

That helmets were not compulsory for so long was utter madness, in retrospect. It was not until 2010 that all hurlers at all grades were obliged to wear them, although they had been made compulsory earlier than that for underage players. The GAA statement announcing this rule change was eager to emphasize the thinking behind it:

> The injuries which the compulsory wearing of helmets will prevent and reduce in numbers are specifically those related to the head, face, eye and dental regions. There are significant

injuries which can be sustained in these areas including scalp lacerations, concussions, skull fractures, jaw fractures, cheekbone fractures, nasal fractures, penetrating eye injury and orbital fractures, facial lacerations and damage to and avulsion of teeth in both the upper and lower jaws.

Alright, alright . . . we get the picture. There has been a massive decrease in those types of injuries, without any lessening of physicality in tight exchanges.

Considering these matters in relation to my own new life as a hurler, I felt I could probably handle the general rough and tumble: Gaelic football had more or less prepared me for that. But the hurleys themselves were a different matter. A hurley is a weapon, and everyone on the field has one, and pretty much everyone on the sideline has one too. I couldn't really think of any of the numerous brawls that I'd been party to in Gaelic football that would have been mollified by the addition of a three-foot ashplant in the hands of all the combatants. I didn't know what to expect when it came to the utilization of this piece of hard, treated wood as a weapon of aggression, but I knew enough to fear it.

Even so, I was rather taken aback by the number of people whose first reaction to the news that I was about to embark on a summer's hurling was to immediately worry for my safety. 'Oh my God, you'll get killed!' This was more than a little disconcerting.

The pull on my knuckles that I got in my first game was sore, certainly. But rather than seeing it as some kind of dark harbinger, I wore the bit of blood and bruising with a degree of pride, if I'm being honest. This was silly, of course, but it was based mainly on the fact that it was a hurling-specific injury, the sort of injury that you just couldn't get on a football field.

If I thought I was going to get the odd slap around the head with a hurley, it didn't sound like fun, but then that was what the helmet was for. As long as I bought even a remotely respectable helmet, then I shouldn't have to worry unduly . . . Right?

In some corner of the Irish public consciousness, hurling is still a game played by bona fide lunatics. And to the outside world, it has at times been even more so.

In *The Gaelic Athletic Association, 1884–2009*, there is a wonderful chapter written by Seán Crosson entitled 'Gaelic Games and "the Movies"'. (Crosson later expanded his work on this chapter into a book called *Gaelic Games on Film*.)

In the article, he describes what Hollywood saw in hurling: a chance to reiterate a few stereotypes of the violent, dangerous, unruly Irish. One 1930s newsreel in particular, the MGM-produced Peter Smith Specialty 'Hurling', had as its major (or sole?) selling point the extreme violence of the sport. In the film posters reproduced in the book, the tagline reads – 'Shillalah's [sic] in Swing Time ... as thirty wild Irishmen demonstrate their game of athletic assault and battery!'

'In all of these depictions,' writes Crosson, 'it is the potential for injury in the game of hurling that is to the fore in the minds of the producers.'

He outlines the extraordinary reaction to a John Ford film, *The Rising of the Moon*, which was shot in Kilkee, Co. Clare, in 1956. The movie has three parts, the second of which is called 'A Minute's Wait'. Two British tourists are on a train that is being repeatedly delayed by various rural Irish calamities. One of these delays is caused by the arrival on the train of the victorious local hurling team, many of whom are carried aboard on stretchers.

The scene caused a furore before shooting had even finished. The *Irish Independent* took a dim view of the content, these hurlers coming back victorious from a game that 'from the appearance of the players must have been bloody and very rough, and hardly played according to the rules of the Gaelic Athletic Association'.

The following day the Director General of the GAA, Pádraig Ó Caoimh, released a statement that he was 'deeply concerned lest there be any substance to this report'. The statement went on to say that Ó Caoimh had been in touch with Lord Killanin, one of the producers of the movie, to clarify the situation, and had been assured that the report of widespread stretcher-carrying was 'exaggerated and completely out of context . . and that in fact there is nothing offensive to our national tradition in this film'.

But that was far from the end of the matter. An official deputation from the Clare County Board went to Kilkee to meet Lord Killanin, and later produced a statement proclaiming that it was

> of grave concern to the GAA that the national game of hurling should, or would appear to be held up to ridicule . . . the matter of fifteen players returning home all suffering injuries would be calculated to give the impression that instead of a national sporting game that they were casualties returning to a clearing station at a battlefield.
>
> Father Corry [the Clare County Board chairman] pointed out that the scene as depicted was completely derogatory to the Gaels of Ireland and to the hurlers in particular. The scene if placed on the screen as filmed would bring the association into disrepute and would be calculated to hold up the national game to ridicule both at home and abroad.

These fevered representations were obviously crying out to be lampooned. The legendary *Irish Times* columnist Myles na Gopaleen stood ready as ever, referring to the 'farcical drool served up by the GAA'. Myles took the opportunity to read the Clare County Board's statement as carried in the *Clare Champion*, noting with interest that on the same page of the *Champion* there was a report from a local hurling game between Ruan and St Joseph's which was described as 'probably one of the worst exhibitions of bad sportsmanship ever seen on a Gaelic field'.

'"There was literally a procession to the Co. Hospital from the match," the Champion's report continued, while "one, a spectator from Ennis, had survived the war in Korea but he almost met his Waterloo in Cusack Park".'

'To many people,' Myles wrote, 'the possibility of vital injury is part of the attraction of hard games . . . the non-belligerent spectators regard absence of such occurrences as an attempt to defraud them. They have paid their two bobs to see melia murdher. Failure to present it is, they feel, low trickery.'

Lord Killanin and John Ford, for their parts, were not too worried about the protestations of the GAA. As Crosson writes: 'Ford appeared in a small part in an Abbey Theatre Irish-language play shortly after the film's production in which "a short passage of Gaelic dialogue was improvised for him". When asked if "he was going back to Spiddal" (the birthplace of his parents) he said he was not as he was "afraid of the GAA".'

None of the games that I played in the summer of 2024 really involved anything untoward. There were, of course, a few bad strokes in every game, but they were all more or less on the ball. We had a few lads who 'didn't spare the timber', but there were no egregious acts of violence, nothing to lead me to doubt my life choices.

After a few games, it was clear to me that there were a lot of benefits to using your hurley to establish personal boundaries. Some of our best ball-carriers would wield the stick pretty freely in the moments before, during, and after catching the ball. Up the arms would go, protecting your chest and the side you were carrying the ball on. This scared me early on, but I began to see the method in it.

What was more worrying was that my own utter naïveté in relation to both the hurley and the sliotar would count against me in some way. If we got involved in a row, and a lad decided to jab the butt of his hurley into my ribs, then I suppose I'd have to deal with that in my own good time. But what really scared me was getting hurt purely because I was too inexperienced or stupid to get out of the way of either a sliotar or a hurley. A hurley could cause damage to you if you didn't know how to tackle or to hook properly; and if you didn't have your wits about you as you went in to close a defender down, you could take a sliotar into the chest or on the arms. An injury incurred doing something as uncoordinated as that would be both painful and humiliating – a combination I was eager to avoid at all costs.

12

My presence was required in Dublin for work the night before our next league game, against De La Salle, and so I drove back on the day of the game, with two stops along the way. It was early evening by the time I reached the house. I had to leave about twenty minutes later to get to the pitch in time. It was the first occasion I'd set off for training or a match where I'd honestly just not felt like it.

Training had been a little better for the past few weeks, but the memory of the Passage game was still fresh in my mind. I had been so useless, so redundant in every possible way, that it was hard to feel anything other than dread about the next match.

I had earmarked this game as a chance for a bit of a family reunion, as it had originally been fixed for a Sunday morning, which would have allowed my uncle Deaglán and a few of his kids, all of whom had once played for De La Salle, to attend. The game had been refixed, which I'd told Deaglán about; cancelled, which I'd also told Deaglán about; and then refixed again for a third date, which I'd forgotten to tell him about. I remembered this only as I was parking the car in An Sean Phobal, and I felt bad about it, but extremely relieved that Deaglán wouldn't be there to witness what I felt sure would be humiliation of a very specific, low-key, low-stakes kind. I had spared him a one-hour drive to discover that his nephew was worse than bad . . . he was an irrelevance.

The team announcement would at least be a relief: surely, this time, I'd be taken out of the line of fire; and then maybe I'd be allowed fifteen minutes at the end, when the game might be a little more stretched. I don't know why I thought the game being more stretched would necessarily be of any use to me. Maybe I just hoped the result would already be decided by then, one way or the other, and I could go about my business in as consequence-free an environment as possible.

The evening was beautiful, but bloody hell I was wrecked. As I was walking into the dressing room, Sean told me we were still down five or six regulars, but we had twenty or twenty-one togging out. That felt like confirmation that I would not be starting.

And then the team was announced, and I was once again at full-forward. For the first time in my life, I was in a GAA dressing room genuinely dreading the game ahead. I just had no enthusiasm left. I was going to be terrible, I was going to be in the way, I was going to be a hindrance to the team winning the game. And I knew it before the game even began.

The warm-up started terribly. I was pucking around with Deccie Ryan and Patrick Conway, the two lads closest in age to me, both of them pure strikers of the ball. They were drilling passes to me that I just couldn't handle. It was dispiriting. I knew they were only trying to get me ready for the game. That's their job, in that moment, and I knew it. But I was not in the mood for these silent home truths to be delivered to me, so I sought out alternative partners for the remaining steps of the warm-up.

Halfway through a possession drill, Sean said something to me that I found very useful. 'When you get the ball in your hand, take your four steps – don't stand. You're a big man, get out of the tackle first, then decide what you want to do with it.' I got a chance to act on this advice almost immediately in the warm-up, and it felt good. Take your steps. Give yourself some space. At least try to be positive.

Once again I took my place at full-forward. Once again I was met with a handshake by a full-back who was built like a fucking mountain.

The opening minutes were spent hoping the ball wouldn't come near me, but ten minutes of that was enough. It dawned on me that I might, in fact, have an aerobic advantage over my marker. This sort of self-talk usually happens in the car on the way to a game, or more annoyingly on the way home, but here it was – wisdom dropping slowly, while the game was on: MOVE!! Don't be a standing target for long balls that you're completely incapable of taking down and doing something with. Just keep running.

Our best forward, Michael Flynn, was playing corner-forward beside me. I knew that I needed to be as far out of his way as possible. So when the ball was in our half-back line, and Michael was close to goal, I drifted out to the 45 to try to pick up short balls. If Michael was playing out the field, as he often tended to, I went deep towards the goalkeeper and then broke out to Michael's wing, to give the other corner-forward some room.

I just kept running. And slowly but surely, things happened around me. Not directly due to my actions, but I had at least become a factor in the game, asking certain tiny questions of the defence. When Michael streaked through for a brilliant goal, I looked at the gap he'd run through and said to myself, 'I could have been standing there, like a big useless ape, but instead I'm out here, forty-five metres from goal, watching an actual hurler scoring.'

With about five minutes to half-time, after I'd had a couple of decent touches, our wing-forward Diarmuid Ó Curraoin picked up a ball along the left wing of our attack and found me with a pass. After the requisite fumbled catch, I had time to pick the ball up and look around. I was forty metres out, about five metres from the touchline. My marker was fifteen metres away. *I'm taking a swing at this*, I said to myself. My arms went so far as to agree with my inner voice. *Yes, on balance, we agree that this is the correct course of action. We'll do our very best to come up with the desired result.*

This back-and-forth duly taken care of, I took another look around to see that the chance hadn't gone. Remarkably, I still had time. There was really nothing else for it but to take my shot: my first attempt at a score since my goal on debut. The connection was weak, but not awful. The ball went wide by about a metre. It wasn't an easy chance, but I was able to plant my feet and hit it. I was annoyed out of my mind that it didn't go over.

Half-time came and all of a sudden I was energized again. We were up a point, and I didn't feel like a complete interloper.

Early in the second half I got another ball about fifty metres out. Cover was too tight to try for a score, and it would have been half over my shoulder anyway. I saw a pass, and I drilled it in to our number 13, Brandon Tobin, who got his score. A couple of minutes later, Michael was standing over a long-distance free. I got to the end-line in case it dropped short and wide, which it did. I put my hurley up to bat it down to myself, and miraculously that's exactly what happened. As I gathered the sliotar, I spotted our wing-back Darragh Healy storming into the penalty area. Against my better judgement, I tried this rather intricate pass – into a space between my marker, who was moving out the field to try and shadow me, and Darragh, who was advancing towards the goal. And it came off! Darragh's shot got blocked but it was another broadly positive contribution – 'the sort of thing that Shane O'Donnell would have done', I said to myself, which was a fairly hilarious method of describing the watery touch down to myself, the fumbled but ultimately successful lift, and the clunky connection the bas of my hurley made with the ball before it somehow made its way to Darragh's hand.

I raced out for another ball a couple of minutes later. It hopped in front of me, skidding off towards my left hand, the hand I hold my hurley in. I tried to reach across my body with my right hand, but it beat me, and my marker, and ended up with the keeper. I should've swapped my hurley over into my right hand, tried to catch the ball with my left, and then swapped back as I tried to take on my man.

As I formulated that thought, it seemed to me that it was a vaguely Hurling Man type of thing to say to yourself. It's not something I'd have had even a passing knowledge of three months ago. This was an error of the sort I could file, alongside the wide I hit in the first half, as a 'hurling error'.

I was taken off a couple of minutes later. In the Passage game, when I was taken off at half-time, I was too ashamed to go near our management, even as they thanked me for my efforts. I was too proud. But this time round, I stood with my uncle John, the subs, and the management, as we ground out a three-point win; our first of the hurling season. And it ranks as one of my top five favourite ever GAA results – An Sean Phobal 3–15 (of which the two Flynn brothers contributed 3–14), De La Salle 1–18. What a joy! And I felt a part of it. You really can't ask for any more than that.

The Tuesday evening after that game, I went training and was marginally better than I'd been at our last hurling session a week before. That's all I could hope for, and on this particular evening it was absolutely sufficient unto the day. So I was feeling generally positive about things as I came up to the turn-off for An Rinn on the R674, when suddenly I could see more or less the entire county of Waterford.

The sea – a breathtaking blue. The coves studding the coastline all the way to Dunmore East. The Coinigéar, a beautiful sandbar stretching from An Rinn to Abbeyside. Dungarvan sitting in its bay in front of the Comeraghs, and behind that the Knockmealdowns bathed in late-evening sunshine. It was a glimpse of the sublime. And there was a feeling – which could have been just emotion, or possibly something deeper – that I had to find a way to spend at least a portion of the rest of my life down here. Rushing between my uncle's house, back and forth to Dublin for work, to get back down here for training – it had all been too hectic for me to actually wrestle with what I was doing this for. It was a stunt for a book. It was also something very precious to me. I rang Dad, and was glad to hear him in brilliant form.

13

Championship week, and for the first time in my career I was not really all that nervous. We'd welcomed a few players back into the fold, we'd been training with about twenty players most nights, and I wouldn't have to worry about another starting jersey unless there was an outbreak of the plague.

The free-takers and forwards were invited down half an hour early for training to practise their shooting, and I was usually there in plenty of time. If I was playing football I'd be practising in this manner, so why not for hurling – Lord knows I needed it. It was interesting to see the older lads tightening up a bit now that championship had arrived. Especially with fellas like Patrick Conway and Declan Ryan, fellas my age, you could see them getting a little narky, a little on-edge. And that's what you want.

I realized on the Thursday evening before training that it had been a full quarter-century since my first adult championship game – and yet the feeling was the exact same.

Sean told me as he was putting the cones out and setting up the session that he first played adult championship football at fourteen (and scored a goal from corner-forward). Tadhg played in a Cork hurling county final at forty-one in goals for Sarsfields. And it's always the same. Even among the young lads who told me they didn't care what the hell Ballyduff were like. 'I don't know, and I don't really care, if I'm honest. All we can do is bring our A-game,' as Andrew Hourigan put it.

Andrew was one of our key figures in defence, and he was still a teenager, playing alongside Luke Wade, our manager's son, who was twenty-one. John Flynn was going to be midfield with Ciarán Ó Mathúna, both of whom were also in their early twenties, and then there was Conor French at centre-forward, who was nineteen. Up front, Marc was under twenty as well, my cousin Cathal was twenty-one, and he would be alongside Michael Flynn, who was just a couple of years older at twenty-three. They were the new heart of the team, and they just couldn't wait to get going.

One evening that week, a man pulled up outside the gate of the cottage. He slowed down to a crawl and lowered his window. 'Young Murphy!' he shouted. I was pretty well used to being hailed by anyone passing along our lonely little bóithrín, so I wandered over to have a chat. His name was Mick Dunford, and he'd heard John Murphy's nephew was staying in the vicinity. 'I knew your grandfather,' he said.

'Well, that's more than I can say for myself – the poor man died eight years before I arrived, on my dad's twenty-sixth birthday. How did you know him?'

'He was a lovely man, I knew him through farming. This might be a little odd . . . but would you have a photo of him by any chance? He was a great fella, but I'm starting to forget what he looked like, and it makes me sad to think I wouldn't be able to remember him.'

That hit me for six, to be honest. And it shook me as well to know that I didn't have a photo of my grandfather Patsy. He was as close a relation to me as my other three grandparents, but they all lived until I was at least ten. I loved them all in different ways, but Patsy was a mystery to me.

I pledged I'd find a photo of Patsy to show Mick Dunford, and I pledged that I'd keep it for myself, too.

Our first game in the championship was fixed for Clashmore on 29 June, a Saturday. This also happened to be the day that Galway were playing Dublin in an All-Ireland football quarter-final in Croke Park. My attitude was that the clash was sparing me from a wasted trip up to Croker. Galway had played four of the last five weekends, Dublin were well rested and focused. I feared a heavy beating for my favourite sports team in the world.

The Galway match would be finishing when we were just entering the final quarter of our game. Best just to put it out of my mind completely.

I got my gear together – water bottles, hurleys, helmet – and off we went. This was the club's first game in the Junior B grade in hurling, and so this was a chance for us to prove we belonged at this level.

That's exactly what we did. Michael Flynn did the majority of our scoring, as he always did, and his brother John was lording it in midfield, despite getting a bit of heavy treatment. One such tackle led to a red card early in the second quarter, by which stage we were already six points up. We led 12 points to 5 at half-time, and we were in total control, so it was a very relaxed half-time warm-up for my fellow subs and me. I was even able to notice that Gill had taken her place on the sideline – she had felt the urge on this particular day to attend her one game for the summer, and had picked the one where she could read her book in the local pub for an hour while we ran through our warm-ups. Then it rained for the first quarter-hour of the match, which would have made staying in the pub more attractive. She made it for half-time, which I took as a Herculean effort on her part.

When I retook my seat for the start of the second half, a young woman had sat down on the bench behind me, a few seats over. She had with her a beautiful golden Labrador, and had spent most of the first half walking her around the pitch. She leaned over a couple of minutes into the second half, and said – 'Ciarán, I'm so sorry. I'm your cousin Patricia – Michael and Ann's daughter. I haven't seen you in twenty-five years or more. I really don't mean to bother you . . . but Galway have just gone two points up on Dublin with about ten minutes left in Croker.'

Holy shit! In a million years, I didn't think Galway were going to do this. But I was here, in Clashmore, with a job to do (such as it was).

'Wow, thanks! Maybe I should just focus on this game, though . . . How are you, by the way?'

'Yeah, no . . . you're right. I should probably just lea–'

'Young Murphy, Dublin have it back to one!' the call came from behind me.

'No, Dec, that's old, they're two up' – another voice entering the chat.

'Galway are two up, with six minutes to play.' That was Patricia's mother Ann, An Sean Phobal's number one supporter, perhaps hoping to draw a line under this sort of undue interruption in our enjoyment of the hurling. The détente lasted for about twenty seconds. There were now four different people updating me, none of whom seemed entirely sure what was going on.

'I have it here on the phone if the 4G will hold up.'

Ah, lads, I might be about to make my championship debut for the club of my forefathers here; I'm trying to focus. And also can we just make sure everyone's information is up to date? This inaccuracy is killing me ... or it would be if I were listening to it, which I'm not. I'm focused, I'm ready. I'm a hurler. A HURLER.

'Dublin are only one down.' Ah, fuck!

'Galway are two up. You're safe, young Murphy.'

'Ah, balls, the internet is patchy.'

'Point Dublin; they're level.'

'Ciarán, warm up there.'

'No, wait, Galway are still up.'

'Game over, Galway have won.'

Wait ... what was that in the middle there? Something about ...

'Ciarán, get your helmet on ... and take off that bloody bib will you, for fuck's sake.'

At the start of the year, Galway beating Dublin in Croke Park in a knock-out football game and me playing a hurling championship game would have both seemed pretty unlikely. And now both of them were happening within seconds of each other. I could have floated onto the pitch. I played the last ten minutes, and a crankier, more contrary version of myself would have been annoyed when a teammate eschewed the option to pass to me when I was directly in front of goal, instead getting his own shot blocked down from an acute angle. But I didn't mind.

Afterwards I sat in the car and headed for the Marine, our local pub and one that will be familiar to anyone who's driven along the main Cork–Waterford road. I couldn't get a hold of my brother Paul, who had been at Croke Park, but I was able to give Dad a rundown on the Old Parish game, in exchange for a summary of Galway/Dublin.

I wouldn't categorize my feelings at this moment as jealousy, but I certainly felt like I'd missed out on something fairly epic. And I certainly would've liked to have had the craic with my Dublin club-mates in Templeogue Synge Street, but hey – you can't have it all.

This was exactly what I was thinking when I walked into the Marine to go drinking with my new teammates ... and instead walked straight into one of the lads from Synger I hadn't seen in six months or more.

'What the hell are you doing here?' we both said to each other.

He was on day two of a wedding in Dungarvan, and the entire wedding party had decamped to the Marine for *ceol agus ól*. I left him to it, and joined my teammates ... and my cousin Patricia.

'Eh, I think we're neighbours in Dublin too, by the way', she told me. It turned out she and her new husband Tom had bought a house no more than 200 metres from our place in Dublin 8. And two of her siblings, another two second cousins of mine, lived no more than a kilometre from there as well.

This world keeps getting smaller and smaller.

14

It became more and more clear as the summer went on that my uncle John was a minister without portfolio. He'd had every job title going in the club, including serving many years as chairman, and was now basically a life member of whatever committee he fancied.

I wanted to talk to him about the history of the club, about what he'd gained from his involvement with the GAA, but we were unfortunately having rather too good a time of it on each occasion I attempted to raise this issue. In the end, I had to depend on the club's unofficial historian, my cousin Michael Hogan's wife Ann, to fill in the gaps.

The summer of 2024 was the fortieth anniversary of the opening of the club grounds in 1984. John was chairman at that time, and he and a couple of others, including his first cousins Michael and Tom, led negotiations to buy a field from a dairy farmer, convert the old creamery into dressing rooms, and give the club a home of its own, after years of using fields granted to them by benevolent locals to host home games.

The club's Facebook page continues the story:

> All the work in levelling the field, picking stones, erecting perimeter fencing, reseeding, planting trees, etc. was done by volunteers, thus making it a viable project. The field was ready to open in 1984 when another great Sean Phobal man, Jimmy French, organized a team to come from New York to play Sean Phobal in the opening fixture on 12th August 1984.
>
> It was a momentous and proud day in the history of our club when we played New York in that opening fixture and over 300 people continued the celebrations in Lawlors Hotel that night to end a never to be forgotten day.
>
> We should never forget and always be grateful to the fantastic committee who gave us the excellent facility we have today. Go raibh maith agaibh go leir. In the midst of our celebrations, at around 3 a.m., word came through that John Treacy from Villierstown had won a silver medal in the Olympic Games when he finished second in the marathon. A great day all round!

Everyone I spoke to about this period of the club's history was serenely matter-of-fact about one thing: the club would not currently exist if it hadn't happened. Old Parish does not have the benefit of a small village, a couple of shops, a few pubs around which to cohere. My home village of Milltown is small, but it is a sprawling metropolis compared with An Sean Phobal.

Maybe it is a case of GAA people being needlessly dramatic when presented with the idea of a life without the GAA, but when locals told me that the entire identity of An Sean Phobal was tied up in the fact that it had a GAA club and ground, it made sense to me.

It's a spectacularly beautiful place, but it's bordered on one side by An Rinn, which has the bustling coláiste full of students every summer, and to the south by Ardmore, another busy beachside town. The place and its GAA club could easily have been subsumed by one or the other – but it has a history all of its own and the GAA club is a way of saying, 'We're going nowhere.'

That's not to say that reality doesn't bite in a million different ways. It's a tiny, tiny club. At underage level it is amalgamated with An Rinn as a club known as An Gaeltacht. The two clubs are amalgamated for female sports as well: the camogie team plays as An Rinn, and the football club is An Sean Phobal. Despite these dilutions – necessary for reasons of numbers – An Sean Phobal are fiercely proud of their independence at men's adult level in football and hurling. Owning their own pitch is a big part of that, and John was a big part of how it happened.

Behind all the jokes and the bravado, he's fiercely proud of it, and everyone in the club is equally proud of everything he did to help bring it to fruition.

John knew my landlord well and asked that I bring him over to our cottage in Kilgobinet one evening, as he wanted to catch up with him. I felt this would be a highly dangerous situation for me, as trying to remove my uncle from the cottage without sharing a few nips of whiskey with him was going to prove difficult.

In the end, I came up with a plan. I was working in Cork one Thursday afternoon, and I said I'd pick him up on the way back and bring him to Kilgobinet, where himself and Paddy could have a chat for a few hours, and then I'd take him back to Old Parish in plenty of time for me to go training that evening.

He would obviously never in a million years stand in the way of me training, so it seemed like the perfect plan. Paddy, Paddy's wife Kathleen, and John had a ball for three hours with Gill and me, and when 6.30 p.m. came I told him I had to leave to get to training. There was no issue getting him in the car, regardless of the four cans of beer he'd had, but once we'd gotten as far as Dungarvan, he inevitably suggested that instead of running him home I run him instead to Mooney's pub in An Rinn for a little nightcap. I said no problem (I had, in fact, foreseen this possibility, and left myself plenty of time to get there and then get to training). When we arrived at Mooney's, he then asked if I'd pop back and run him home after training. Again, this would be no problem whatsoever.

When I landed back to Mooney's just after 9 p.m.,

he was engaged in about three different conversations simultaneously, most of them involving the ongoing seventy-year rivalry between An Sean Phobal and An Rinn. I settled in for the long haul.

He said he'd just finish the pint in front of him. At 10.30, I suggested that he might have one more, and at 11 p.m. I finally managed to extricate him from the premises. He had the whole place in stitches for the couple of hours I was there, and my second cousin Aoife behind the bar was laughing pretty hard too.

On the drive home he was telling me about his other passion, besides the local GAA club: amateur dramatics. For a tiny village, An Sean Phobal has an impressively vibrant theatrical tradition, and John has been integral to that too. As with all true superstars, it can be difficult for the audience to differentiate between the actor and the roles he plays. John had already experienced this uncomfortable situation. His appearances are usually show stoppers, no matter what the precise requirements of the role are, and they are accompanied by raucous laughter.

He had very nearly won an All-Ireland medal for Scór in the novelty act section. Scór is basically the GAA's cultural wing – a competition devised along the usual club lines, but instead of hurling or football, they compete at county, provincial, and then national level in areas like set-dancing, instrumental music, solo-singing, quizzes . . . and novelty acts, little ten-minute plays, usually humorous or at least humour-adjacent. An Sean Phobal had got painfully close to national honours in one such drama, with John in the role of an elderly gentleman. In the notes taken by the adjudicators were written the words 'Old Man excellent', and John has since taken this review as a kind of North Star.

The night of our first hurling championship win, I was in the pub with him and told him it would be my honour to one day tread the boards together. This was passed along the chain of command with devastating speed, to the extent that by the time I had left the pub I had already been informed that the next play had been selected, and auditions would begin shortly. And so, in the midst of the hurling championship, I found myself in the Halla Colmán in the village, taking my seat for my first ever acting audition.

The play was written by our twenty-one-year-old midfielder John Flynn, a drama student in UCC, and his mother Helen, and the three main parts would be played by John himself, our young centre-back Andrew Hourigan, and Conor French. My first cousin Bríd's daughter Doireann would be in it too. It was a War of Independence romance, featuring a Protestant girl, a Catholic boy freshly back from the First World War trenches, and plenty of IRA intrigue. It was written with such vitality and verve, such a feel for the sweep of the times, that I was just bowled over by it. John had given me a copy of the script before training the week before, and I had already given it a couple of reads by the time we got ourselves in a circle for the read-through. The part he had in mind for me was as a local RIC constable, who looked on John and company as foolish young men playing with fire and unwilling or unable to reckon with the consequences of their actions.

I got to call my young teammates 'delinquent scum' and do a bit of grandstanding, and it was great fun – but once they started talking about the amount of rehearsal time required, I knew I was going to be in trouble. They were looking to work through the autumn and into the winter before going on stage in January, and although Gill and I were already dreaming about relocating down here permanently, that would not be happening in time to allow me to take a part in the play. Eventually, I had to bow out.

There also wasn't a role suitable for my uncle in the production, and that was another factor in my decision: I would have very much enjoyed watching his artistic process. But it was so heartening to see a tiny rural parish producing a script written by someone from the village, for the third year in a row, and giving everyone with any ambitions in that direction the chance to flex their theatrical muscles. Plenty of villages have drama societies, but not many have that level of engagement at the creative level. And fewer still have their standout hurling midfielder, in his early twenties, writing and starring in productions.

I was wondering afterwards why I had been so sorely tempted to try the acting. It came back to that line my friend Clare gave me, about not being afraid to be terrible at something in your forties. I was in danger of becoming addicted to the idea of finding that perfect moment of total failure.

15

We'd gotten off to a flying start in our five-team hurling championship group with that win first day out. We didn't have a game scheduled on the second weekend of the championship, so we decided to get ourselves a challenge match, against Midleton in Cork. It would be against a mix of their second and third teams, but Midleton is a big town, and there's only one club in it, so they were a little too good for us. Again I came on for the last ten minutes, and again got the sum total of zero touches, but I was feeling extremely phlegmatic about things. In the end, I was there, wasn't I – and that was the main thing.

I drove home. When I walked in the door of the cottage, Gill was there to greet me.

'Well, how did you get on?'

'Oh, lost by five or six in the end.'

'Did you get on?'

'Just for the last few minutes. Didn't get a touch, would you believe.'

'So what, are you going to be the team mascot now? Sparky the mascot, dressed up like a big lightning bolt, is that the plan?'

'Ehhh . . . no. It's just the Ó Mathúna brothers are back fit now, there's a ton of better players down there.'

'Alright so, Sparky, if that's what you really think.'

The name-calling continued for a little longer than strictly necessary for her to make her point . . . but she'd nevertheless delivered it with pinpoint accuracy.

For nearly twenty years, she was used to seeing me come home from training, giving out about my performance, giving out about a lack of effort on the part of teammates, giving out about managers, or just generally giving out. She had seen me cancel plans, rearrange weekends away, and put Gaelic football first, no matter how much inconvenience it involved. The one thing she had never seen me do was drift along serenely. So to see me come home after having not gotten a touch in a game, and for me to greet this news with a shrug of the shoulders, caused her no end of amusement.

There was something I had to admit to. I was far, far too happy down here – I was too busy planning the rest of my life to really focus on my hurling. It had been my birthday the week before, and we'd had our best friends down, along with their kids. The weather had been beautiful, the children had run around our yard and the country lanes surrounding the house, looking at cows and sheep and horses. We'd eaten in Dungarvan, had pints in Lismore and Ardmore and An Rinn . . . the whole week had been lifted straight out of a Rockshore ad.

This was living . . . but it was not elite high performance. Gill had been speaking in jest, but it hit home. If I'm not making the team, and I'm not making any impact on the games when I come on as a sub, where's my desire to get better? Where's the anger, for want of a better word? The truth was, I had yet to dredge up any so far.

There were sound tactical reasons for my general approach on the pitch – basically doing whatever I could to stay out of Michael Flynn's and Marc Ó Mathúna's way. But my reasons for doing so were not wholly altruistic. I was also a little afraid to fail. The truth is that I was rather too pleased with myself and my small achievements – playing a few league games, getting championship minutes, and the very occasional useful touch. The stunt had already come off. The danger was that I'd just let it meander along.

There was another thing I had to face up to: my hand still hurt like a fucker after every training session. I had to start wearing the glove. No more nonsense. I needed to get angry, play angry, and stay angry. And no number of pints in the sunshine or dips in the ocean were going to change my mind.

A normal person might feel that anger – manufactured anger – was not the healthiest reaction to my situation. But despite dramatic advances in sports psychology, Irish sportspeople (and GAA people in particular) remain wedded to the idea that some white-hot kernel of bitterness is necessary for high performance. And it seems I am no exception.

I'm having the best summer of my life, and as a GAA player I'm not gonna take it any more. At least that's what I had to keep telling myself.

As I said to Gill amidst her barrage of sarcasm, the Ó Mathúna brothers were back, and that meant that I played with Marc for the first time. He was the Old Parish man on the Waterford under-20 team from earlier in the year, and he'd been rehabbing a knock since then. He'd even taken my place in the dressing room by the time I'd arrived for the game against Midleton that evening, the sort of naked power-play which, let's face it, he really didn't have to engage in. (He obviously didn't have a clue where I'd been sitting for the previous three months, but I liked the feeling of relevance it gave me to see him sitting there.)

It's not easy for a fella like Marc to come back from playing under-20 for his county to a Junior B hurling team, and a player in a situation like that can get caught between two stools. He can try and do too much for the club side, which looks like selfishness, or he can try and play his own game, within the team system, and be accused of not taking on enough responsibility. How Marc handled it was going to define our season, but one thing was obvious – the kid could hurl. He was just effortlessly good. And given the magic that Michael Flynn had already delivered in every game we'd played so far, I was struggling to see many Junior B teams with a pair of forwards as good as those two.

Added to that was the fact that they both had a brother playing midfield; the Flynn/Ó Mathúna dynamic was at the very heart of the whole team. With those guys firing, far from being candidates to go straight back down, we could aim for much higher.

The following Thursday night at training, I slipped the glove on as surreptitiously as I could in the dressing room and headed out onto the field. No alarms were raised, no fingers pointed in scorn. It was all so much better, immediately. It turns out that actually wanting the ball to come in your direction has a positive impact on your chances of getting possession. I had rung my buddy Cormac in Dublin after Gill's mascot jibes. I've played football with Cormo for the last seven years as we advanced into our forties together. He laughed uproariously. 'Thank Christ for her. I wouldn't think much of you as a footballer if you acted like it didn't matter to you. Why the hell would we still be playing in our forties if it didn't matter to us? If you've got comfortable, make yourself uncomfortable. I wouldn't rate you as a man if you didn't. And make someone else uncomfortable. Don't be the worst man at training the next night. Start picking lads off. Don't be in the bottom three on Thursday night.'

I thought it was at least arguable that I avoided being in the bottom three that night. Whether that had anything to do with the fact that we were playing championship in two days' time, and therefore everyone else was absolutely taking it handy, was a question I decided not to ruminate upon too deeply. When I got chances to go through on goal, I wasn't apologetically hitting it into the ground – I put my back into it and really struck the thing like I meant it. In first-touch drills, I was running full-pelt onto the ball, not waiting for it to come to me. If you make a mistake, make it at top speed. It was all about attitude, and I had brought a bit to training.

Our second championship group game, against Abbeyside, had the potential to be very tough for us, but in the end Michael Flynn and Marc were exceptional. We were 2–10 to 0–8 ahead at half-time having been facing into the breeze, and we played some powerful stuff. I got on for five minutes at the end, and three forwards had been brought on before me, but obviously I could have no complaints – it was a properly strong squad now. And with two wins from two in the group, we were all of a sudden in a commanding position. Forget about going back down, we were suddenly in the mix for another promotion. There would be no more room for experimentation, no more room for sentiment. If my improvement was to continue, it would have to be measured at training.

Our next game was the following weekend, against

Kilgobinet. They had struggled in their opening two games, and we were heavily favoured to win. Sean had detected a change in my approach to training, and on the Wednesday night he'd said that I should prepare myself to see a bit of game-time. 'You're flying it, lad. We'll see how we go but we'd like to give you a good spell on the field and give you a proper chance to get stuck in.'

This Kilgobinet fixture put me in the odd position of playing for one tiny parish against the tiny parish in which I was residing, at least for one more week until we moved to our new place back in An Sean Phobal. I'd been talking to my landlord and he told me up-front that Kilgobinet's full-back was 'a hatchet man, plain and simple'. This may well have been the oldest trick in the book, intended to intimidate me, but of course it stuck in my mind.

I was pumped, I was ready to rumble. I'd spent less time in my car that week than I had all summer. I'd tried to do everything right to get myself into the best possible shape ... and then, with the warm-up moments away from being finished, my back went into spasm. I get little back niggles all the time, but I knew straight away this was different. I was down on the turf within seconds.

It was the first time, really, that my age had been a factor. Being a novice had made me feel like a youngfella, and up to this point my fitness had been fine. But as the pain went shooting from my crocked lower back along the length of my left leg, the message was clear: I was old. This is the way of things after forty. Your body cooperates until it doesn't. Instead of grabbing my hurley and getting a chance to carry whatever bit of anger and contrariness I'd been trying to cultivate for a fortnight, I was using it as a crutch. It was a proper sickener.

I suspected immediately that I would be missing a great opportunity, and so it proved. We got a healthy lead and ran the bench in the last twenty minutes. Everyone seemed to get a run, everyone seemed to get a score or two. I felt I'd missed a big chance to feel like a hurler, just once, in the heat of a championship.

With three wins from three, we had qualified outright with a game to spare. But with top spot in the group still up for grabs, there probably wouldn't be any more chances to get lads some game-time. Top spot meant you went straight to the West Waterford semi-final, while the teams in second and third would qualify for preliminary quarter-finals. It would be all business from here on out.

16

The morning after the Kilgobinet game, Gill drove me up to Dublin for the All-Ireland hurling final. I had been planning to drive up by myself, but I was in no fit state to get behind the wheel.

I didn't feel I could say I'd immersed myself in hurling for a summer without being present for the All-Ireland final. It's not like I hadn't been before – I'd been to plenty – but this one would surely hit a little differently.

The inter-county hurling season had been exceptional for large parts, the poor-quality games had been glossed over in the usual fashion, and for the first time since 2019 Limerick were not in the final. Their attempt to win an unprecedented five All-Ireland hurling titles in a row had been ended by Cork in the semi-final, in a repeat of their match earlier in the year in Páirc Uí Chaoimh that had been nearly every bit as good.

In the same way that the Kerry footballers had to get used to every game they lost being called a classic for large parts of their history, these Limerick hurlers have had to accept that people are eager for new teams to come along. The level of interest in Clare/Cork had been outrageous, the scramble for tickets had been a blood sport, and the nation was ready to tune in and see new champions.

The Second Captains summertime season on RTÉ Radio 1 had started that week too, and at the end of that first show we replayed a reading by Theo Dorgan, who had been with us in the studio the year before. He had read his poem 'All-Ireland Final' for us, and it summed up quite accurately the level of excitement that seemed to be general around the country:

We stand for the anthem, buoyant and tribal, heart beating with heart,
our colours brave, our faces turned from the uncertain sun.
The man beside me takes my hand, good luck to yours, he says;
I squeeze his calloused palm and then – he's gone.
A shadow socket where he was, the man beside him vanishes
and another before me, behind me; all around Croke Park
one by one we wink out of existence: tens, hundreds, then
thousands, the great arena emptying out, the wind curling in
from the open world to gather us all away. Each single one of us.
I could feel myself fail at the end, but then maybe everyone thought that,
each one of us the last to go. The whistle blew and we all
came back with a roar, everything brighter and louder, desperate and vivid.
I held his hand a moment longer, I wished his team all the luck in the
   world.

I was in the press box at the front of the upper deck of the Hogan Stand, and so was able to enjoy pretty much the best view in the house. It can be a strange place to watch a game sometimes. It can feel like an oasis of relative calm in a maelstrom, but you're also never too far from the general public, and if the atmosphere is good, you don't feel at a remove from it.

And from the off, the game was properly frenetic. Inside the first twelve minutes Cork's Robert Downey caught a puck-out on his own 65-metre line, ran the ball sixty metres, and then hammered home a shot off his hurley that looked set to go down in All-Ireland folklore . . .

. . . but it ended up a footnote, because about halfway through the second half, Tony Kelly embarked on a slaloming run that finished with him scoring for Clare just about the greatest goal ever seen in an All-Ireland hurling final. There were a variety of touches off his hurl that people cooed over endlessly, but his second-last touch was the one that elevated the score to something that almost defied belief. He had set up a flicked finish with the touch before that, but he still had the presence of mind to take another, minuscule touch, to make absolutely sure the ball was where he needed it to be for him to flick it home. It was a tiny adjustment, done at top speed, with four defenders around him and a goalkeeper charging towards him. It was like an Olympic gymnast making a course-correction in mid-air, a guitarist reacting on the hoof as a string breaks. It was utterly, utterly sensational. If you hadn't caught it in real time, the TV replays in the stadium drew repeated gasps.

Kelly described it in a weirdly matter-of-fact way in the press conference afterwards:

> Yeah, just there was a couple of red bodies and I was trying to avoid them and take my point. Often goals are made by the defender rather than yourself. You don't take the ball and think, 'I am going to score a goal here.' It's often that you take what is in front of you really, so when the defender came I didn't want to get blocked down, so I had to sidestep him and then another defender came so I had to sidestep again. And once you're through you have to have a rattle at a goal.

Maybe this is modesty, of the kind with which we are very familiar in sport. The bigger the star, the harder it seems to get them to actually describe what they've just done. The GAA might be a world leader in this area. But the bit Kelly focuses on are the sidesteps, relatively unremarkable in comparison to the two delightful touches off his hurley. Maybe that's what he thought was the hard bit about the goal — a small man wrong-footing men far larger than him. To Tony Kelly, maybe those astounding touches are like tying your shoelaces. He was just getting the sliotar where he needed it in order to score a goal.

This was a perfect example of what Jamie Wall had told me after the game in Cappoquin in May: 'Hurling is not a thinking man's game.' Every part of what Tony Kelly did in the build-up to the goal was on instinct. Every quarter of a second brought a different parameter to take into account. It was a chance for a point, until it wasn't — and then it became a goal chance. Kelly's genius (and the genius of the game as a whole, I suppose) is meeting the moment with the required action.

It feels pointless to try to describe what distinguished the 2024 All-Ireland final from any previous All-Ireland final I'd attended, given my new frame of reference. I had never attended a hurling match in Croke Park and thought, 'Well this all seems pretty straightforward.' I had always had deep respect for the artistry required. But that respect went through the roof here.

Everywhere, the ball fizzed from hurley to hand. Every tiny handling error was punished. The speed of the game was bewildering. The composure required to hit long-range scores after you've run seventy or eighty metres to get some space. The performances of so many players under the most exquisite pressure, for almost a hundred minutes including extra time, were breathtaking.

Shane O'Donnell's ability to insinuate himself into the game after a very quiet opening quarter — and playing, as we learned later, on an injured hamstring – was a mark of sheer bravery, commitment, skill, and patience. He set up Clare's first goal for Aidan McCarthy by regaining the ball in the tackle and then somehow finding a pass through a thicket of bodies. Later, he scored two points in a couple of minutes when Clare desperately needed them. Playing on one leg, he was still virtually unmarkable.

I went to Fagan's on Drumcondra Road to meet Jamie after the game, and ended up in conversation with Shane O'Donnell's brother, who was looking more than a little dazed at what had just unfolded. When emotions are as heightened as they are at All-Ireland finals, you're never entirely sure of the quality of what you've just watched, but consensus was growing that this was one of the great ones.

RTÉ's coverage drew an audience of over one million, exceeding the figure that would watch the football final a week later. The BBC in their infinite wisdom had for the first time broadcast the final live across the entirety of the UK on BBC2.

For the 2024 season, the finale of which I had just watched, only eleven counties competed for the Liam MacCarthy Cup, and Antrim was the only one from north of Athlone. But judging by those audience figures, at least *watching* the All-Ireland hurling final is an all-Ireland pastime.

Maybe the fact that half the country dedicates itself to

a sport as hard to learn as hurling is the real achievement. The Hurling Man manages to hold both of these truths simultaneously: it's a travesty that more people don't play it, and it's a miracle that it's played at all.

17

An Sean Phobal's status as a dual club carried for me a certain weight, a certain status. In the same way that I felt a degree of smugness about being a dual player, it seemed to me that a club should be entitled to stick its chest out and say, 'We are offering all the meats of the GAA stew here. What's your excuse?'

Looked at from outside the GAA bubble, it is a miracle possibly unmatched in world sport to have one indigenous game, Gaelic football, embedded in rural communities across Ireland, more often than not outperforming a pair of global sports with massive footprints, rugby and Association football.

But I prefer to look at it another way. If you were drawing up the ideal circumstances in which you could conceivably try to double the number of people playing hurling, a singularly magnificent sport, you would do well to find better conditions for it to thrive, in principle, than exist in the GAA currently. The physical, social, and cultural infrastructure – clubs that are deeply rooted in communities and that offer players of all ages the chance to represent their home place – already exists. And I firmly believe that we should be doing everything in our power to help hurling grow beyond its current strongholds.

Liam Griffin managed Wexford to their last All-Ireland hurling title in 1996. He has been a tireless advocate for the game, and its most trenchant critic. He might best be described as hurling's conscience. When the game's been good, Griffin has no equal in his description of its beauty. When it falls short of what he envisions it to be, he remorselessly tries to improve it.

In the spring of 2023, Griffin introduced a motion to GAA Congress, advocating that every club field at least one hurling team at under-7 and/or under-9 grade, and that every county organize hurling games on the Go Games model for those grades. (Go Games has been a hugely successful initiative to get young children playing GAA, where no score is kept, subs are rolled on and off constantly, and the emphasis is on participation, not winning.) The motion got only 34.6 per cent support in 2023 – well short of the 60 per cent required for passage but enough to allow him to bring it back to Congress two years later.

When I spoke to him ahead of the 2025 Congress, he was trenchant in his view that every child in Ireland should get the chance to hold a hurley and learn the basics. In the sort of straightforward language for which he is renowned, he told me that Kate Middleton (in one of those rather unimaginative Croke Park visit photos) got more of a chance to play hurling than a lot of Irish kids.

Beyond the scope of his motion to Congress, Griffin has also been arguing that if you are given the chance to play hurling as a kid, you should also then be given a clear road-map to keep playing into adulthood. If your own club doesn't have adult hurling teams, then we should make it easy for adults to play football for one club and hurling for another. In certain counties, including in Griffin's Wexford, that is currently not allowed. As Griffin put it to me, you can walk into any rugby club or soccer club in Ireland, pay your registration fee, and play away. But if you're a member of a Gaelic football club, that in itself might be enough to stop you from playing hurling.

Griffin travelled to Donegal for Congress in 2025, and then decided to withdraw the motion. On the face of it, this seemed most un-Griffin-like behaviour. I rang him a couple of days afterwards to ask him about it.

He told me that he had seen a window of opportunity. He had been told that the GAA's new Hurling Development Committee had given his motion unanimous support. Griffin was now happy to hand the idea over to the HDC, and to the new National Head of Hurling, Willie Maher, who would take up his role later that spring, in April

2025. Jarlath Burns, the GAA president, had also given the motion his unqualified support. Griffin had attended enough GAA Congresses over the years to have a pretty good sense of when he was being fobbed off and when he was being listened to. And he was happy to put his trust in the HDC to take his idea on board and wrap it into whatever suite of proposals they would finally come up with to try to grow the game of hurling.

It was an interesting time for Griffin to be wrestling with such things. At that time, in early 2025, the entire GAA community had been watching as a Football Review Committee, headed by Jim Gavin, brought about fundamental change in how Gaelic football is played – all in under twelve months. It was proof that the oil tanker of GAA democracy could be turned round much more quickly than anyone had previously thought possible. Time may well make a mockery of Griffin's faith in the potential of the HDC to expand the accessibility of hurling. But it has more power to deliver change than a Congress motion introduced by his club in Wexford, and Griffin knew it.

Talking to Liam Griffin about the game, a picture of the three Rackard brothers sitting prominently on his desk, is an incredibly enriching way to spend an hour. He is by turns funny, angry, acerbic, and despairing. But when we spoke at length before Congress 2025, he had no truck whatsoever with counties that do not do enough for hurling.

This raises an obvious question: are the geographical limitations of hurling country rooted in some sort of historical inevitability?

If an American tourist sat down beside an Irish person in a Dublin bar and asked where the hell the sport they were watching on TV comes from, chances are that Cúchulainn would probably be mentioned before too long. That has power. It is one of the things that sets the game apart from the other popular field sports in Ireland. It is one of the reasons that UNESCO added hurling to the Representative List of the Intangible Cultural Heritage of Humanity in 2018.

In the 1870s and 1880s, the differences between rugby, Association football, and Gaelic football were not very well defined. There was just enough historical evidence of an Irish ball game throughout the seventeenth and eighteenth centuries for the GAA to claim Gaelic football as a sport unique in the world, but we all know that it's part of a family that includes not just rugby and soccer but also Aussie rules and the NFL. An Irish version of football was a handy thing to have in the 1880s, when the GAA took its place among the other elements of the Irish Cultural Revival, but it is pointless to try to minimize its kinship with other ball sports.

Hurling, on the other hand, could be traced back to some of the foundational folk-tales of human life on the island, and the GAA's founding fathers were never shy in mentioning that, given the political climate of the time.

Whatever Cúchulainn was doing, we are eager to call it hurling, even though he was knocking around as an individual, not as part of a team. (He hardly needed teammates when, as we are reliably informed, he was taking on and beating 150 boys at his uncle's court at Emain Macha.) Various ball-and-stick games – camánacht in Scotland and the Isle of Man, bandy in Wales, Sautreiben in the Rhineland, Hurmussen in Switzerland – show some kinship with hurling. If you'd sat down to watch Martin Scorsese's *Killers of the Flower Moon* in 2023, you would have seen Native American children trying to get Leonardo di Caprio involved in a game that looks an awful lot like ground hurling.

But none of these games retains anything close to the cultural force that hurling has in this country, and modern ball-and-stick games like cricket and hockey bear little or no meaningful relation to hurling. Meanwhile, what has happened since the GAA set about reviving and codifying hurling is genuinely miraculous. If hurling looked quite a bit like hockey for most of its history, it has gone off on another evolutionary path entirely over the past 140 years or so. And it is the magnificence of the game that has evolved over that time, far more than its deep roots in the mists of Irish antiquity, that justifies all efforts to expand its limited geography.

In the seventeenth and eighteenth centuries, antecedents to the modern game of hurling were played with the enthusiastic support of some of Ireland's landed gentry, who sponsored teams made up of their tenants and whoever else they thought might be useful. After the 1798 Rebellion and the Act of Union, the gentry moved away from their sponsorship of hurling and transferred their interest to cricket. Not coincidentally, cricket was the most popular field sport in Ireland in the 1870s, on the eve of the GAA's foundation.

Hurling's decline in the nineteenth century can be attributed to a number of factors, including agrarian agitation and the Famine. The game at home was in need of a saviour when Michael Cusack came along.

In Paul Rouse's peerless *The Hurlers*, he finishes his description of the first ever meeting of the Gaelic Athletic Association in Hayes' Hotel in Thurles thus:

> Hurling had, until now, lived outside the world of modern sport in Ireland, but that had now changed. What happened next transformed the game, and assured it of a future. Many years later, in his dying days, when he cast an eye back on his motivation for founding the GAA, Michael Cusack offered a succinct summary: 'I resolved to bring back the hurling.' This wasn't all that motivated him – but it proved to be his crowning glory.

So what exactly had Cusack set out to save? This is not at all easy to answer. Thinking about what hurling was in the centuries before it was codified by the GAA is a bit like playing pool in a pub anywhere in Ireland and querying whether they play back-table or not . . . or whether you have to shout the pocket you're going to pot the black into. Local rules and customs are just that – local. Sports in the 1800s can't be siloed as definitively as we'd like and as hurling has been.

The more pressing questions, for those of us who wish to see hurling expand, are these: Why is hurling country so geographically limited? And how much does that historical geography matter today?

As we have seen, the historian Kevin Whelan developed a plausible geographical theory for why hurling thrived on the best agricultural land in Ireland, while football flourished pretty much everywhere else. But it would be absurd to argue that rushy or rocky topography is an obstacle to the growth of hurling today.

The history of hurling in Kilkenny – which has for some decades been seen as the quintessential hurling county – is instructive in helping us get beyond ideas of geographical inevitability. Kilkenny was a cricket county, and then a football county, before the early All-Ireland successes of 1904 and 1905 set them off on a century of hurling success. The historian Mark Duncan has written about this surprising trajectory:

> In the late nineteenth century, hurling was far from Kilkenny's most popular sport. The game was certainly played, but

not always to a standard that would endear it to the knowledgeable onlooker. Michael Cusack was one such onlooker. The GAA's founder and principal propagandist had visited Kilkenny city in April 1887 and did little to conceal his disgust at what he saw.

Writing in the pages of his own newspaper, the *Celtic Times*, Cusack voiced his dismay at the 'pale, emaciated' figures he encountered while walking through the streets of the city. On the steps of the Bank of Ireland, for instance, he observed a 'crowd of persons, who probably call themselves men, slothfully reclining with their faces towards the sun', while 'the huge pillars of the town hall supported the dead weight of a lot of fellows'.

Cusack's mood didn't lighten when he reached the hurling field. There, a poorly attended game was being played out between two teams whose hurling was 'the worst and most spiritless ever witnessed on an Irish hillside'. At one point, as the game continued around them, a half dozen players took to lying on the ground to take a rest. It was, Cusack raged, a 'contemptible perversion' of the ancient game and enough to break the hearts of the more serious hurling folk to be found in Galway or Tipperary.

The first ever game of Gaelic football under the GAA's newly minted rules was played in Kilkenny in February 1885. (Kilkenny is now, of course, the only county that does not compete for the All-Ireland football championship.)

And cricket remained the most popular sport in the county up until the turn of the twentieth century. A ban on the playing of 'foreign' games by GAA members, re-introduced in 1902, forced the many cricketers in Kilkenny to choose one game or the other. In the political climate of the time, patriotism prevailed.

There are other chinks in the notion that geography was the sole determinant of hurling's success or failure. Hurling thrived in Donegal in the pre-GAA era, but was let down by the length of time it took for a county board to be formed there. When the GAA finally came into being in 1905, Donegal was the last county to have a formal GAA structure in place. They won the first of their three Ulster hurling titles the following year, but that county board lapsed after two years, and did not re-form until 1919. Would there still be hurling in Donegal if there had been a GAA infrastructure capable of growing whatever seeds of the game had already been sown there before Michael Cusack came along? We will never know.

In the mid-1990s, the Ulster hurling officer said that he would have a better chance promoting cricket in south Armagh than hurling. The point, I think, was not that people in south Armagh were intrinsically fonder of cricket than of hurling (though this may be true of Oisín McConville). The point was that hurling was a tougher nut to crack precisely because it was competing for GAA oxygen with Gaelic football. As long as that logic prevails, hurling will struggle to grow.

As it happens, the current GAA president, Jarlath Burns, comes from south Armagh. After Liam Griffin spoke at the GAA Congress in February 2025, the way in which Burns addressed the issues Griffin's advocacy had put on the agenda suggested times might be changing.

'Joe McDonagh [a former GAA president] talked about aspirational rhetoric,' Burns said. 'We're very good at it, the words "we must". We have to move out of our comfort zone. The biggest opposition to [the growth of] hurling is Gaelic football and Gaelic football attitudes. We have to own up to it.'

If hurling was stymied by rugby or soccer around the country to the extent that its own association's president says it is stymied by Gaelic football, we'd probably be mentioning 'garrison games', 'perfidious Albion', and other boring, pointless epithets. But the reality of the dynamic is fairly dull. The running of even a medium-sized Gaelic football club demands a number of things. It needs committed trainers and coaches at youth level; an inexhaustible number of hours on the pitch with teams; and, at the sharp end of adult competition, eight or nine months of hard training, singularity of focus, sacrifice, and bloody-mindedness.

In truly dual clubs, hurling halves the time available for football and doubles the obstacles to success. Focus gets lost. Whatever about an historically dual club, trying to bring hurling (or indeed football) into a successful one-code senior club now would present massive issues for already time-poor club administrators. People in those clubs might well be in favour of the promotion of hurling in principle, but not to the detriment of football.

This mindset is not, of course, restricted to club level. Michael Duignan had barely retired as an Offaly hurler when he took over the job as Meath hurling manager in November 2001. In his first season, 2002, Meath beat Carlow and Laois in the Leinster championship, the county's best results in hurling in years.

But the following year, he encountered significant opposition at every turn from his county board. Rather than looking to build on the success he'd led Meath to the previous year, they repeatedly fixed club football league games for the same weekend as inter-county hurling games. Given that most of the inter-county hurlers were also club footballers, this was a hostile statement of intent by a strong football county. Duignan and his team of selectors were so incensed at the county board's refusal to refix club football games that they walked away from their roles in the week before a crucial hurling league game against Antrim in April 2003. They were prevailed upon to return and finish out the season, but Duignan never hid his disgust at how hurling was treated in Meath.

Talking to Duignan now, he still sees much of the same

attitude. He had been asked in early 2025 to help one prominent football county to come up with a plan to grow hurling beyond its current couple of pockets of clubs. They had business people on board, they had a structure, they had reasonable, achievable goals . . . but they couldn't get help from either their provincial council or their own county board.

That county board, like many others, is spending a lot of money on the preparation of their inter-county football teams. The arms race to stay relevant in football kills whatever altruistic desire might be latent in GAA people to see their hurling team promoted from, say, the fourth tier to the third tier. Reaching the level of the Laois hurling team, for example, might be *achievable*. But is it *desirable* for enough GAA people, in those counties?

This zero-sum thinking cuts both ways, of course. Think of that famous, possibly apocryphal line from Christy Ring about the most beneficial thing that could happen to Cork hurling – 'a knife through every football east of Bandon'. The two biggest dual counties in the country also happen to be the two largest counties in Ireland by area. Cork and Galway are big enough to have football- and hurling-exclusive areas within their county boundaries, which allows clubs to get on with focusing on their preferred sport without preventing the county from fighting for the All-Ireland on two fronts. Other counties, perhaps inevitably, tack firmly in one direction or the other.

Are dual clubs and counties the only true Gaels out there? I wouldn't put it as strongly as that. The GAA never required that clubs offer both football and hurling, and the logic of that omission filtered up to inter-county level. But seeing a club like Old Parish, with such a tiny playing population, going from one to the other as if it's the most natural thing in the world, with almost entirely the same playing squad, was instructive for someone like me who'd never experienced it before.

Of course, Old Parish is not a blueprint for clubs in places with little or no tradition of hurling. The popularity and prominence of hurling in the county of Waterford made it far easier for An Sean Phobal to restart hurling in the club. If hurling is to grow significantly, it needs to do so in the large swathes of the country where it has never been played at any scale.

I think Griffin is right to focus on creating some kind of hurling infrastructure for the youngest GAA members. If you start 'em young, you have a chance of holding on to them. Also, global study after global study tells us that children benefit from playing a wide range of sports. Broadening a child's range of sporting experience within your own Gaelic football club is the most risk-free bit of experimentation imaginable if you're a GAA person.

Thinking about what can be done regarding older cohorts, I consider if there's anything to be gleaned from how I came to be sitting on a bench in Clashmore, about to make my hurling championship debut, aged forty-one years and eleven months. I try to take myself back to the Phoenix Park with my friends, walking in the steps of Michael Cusack in January of 1884, hitting the ball back and forth to each other for, as Jack Lynch said at Christy Ring's graveside, 'the sheer thrill of the feel and the tingle in their fingers of the impact of ash on leather', and I wonder why that is not a natural part of life across the whole of this small island.

To me, there's a simple poetry in it — like a father and son playing catch in the backyard in America. It's a stationary, easy, rhythmic, beautiful way to spend half an hour. If every Gaelic football club had a barrel in their back room, along with the bibs and cones, and filled that barrel with hurleys and sliotars and a helmet or three, I'm sure that under-16 and minor and under-20 footballers wouldn't be long waiting to try it out. There is a long-standing tradition of kids hanging around local GAA pitches kicking balls, practising their skills, and using them as places to spend time with friends. The provision of hurleys and sliotars by clubs as a gateway into the game would give the venture the official seal of approval that my abortive puck-around on the local pitch with my dad back in the early 1990s so obviously lacked.

It would be an alternative route into the game. And even if it never went beyond a puck-around for the vast majority, at least you could say that they were engaging with the sport on some level other than just being a supporter.

Anyone who has coached young Gaelic footballers knows that turning up is 95 per cent of the battle. Whether you played Gaelic football to a high level or not is immaterial. There is a belief that hurling is different – that it cannot be coached at under-9 level by someone who has never played the game. That's understandable, but it's misguided. If games promotions officers are made available to clubs, you'll always find parents willing to help set out drills and facilitate the playing of the game.

Since September 2024, clubs have been able to apply to the Hurling Development Committee for starter packs to help them set up hurling in their clubs. (Over 100 clubs applied, including eleven from Louth alone, Willie Maher told me.)

When Denis Walsh reported from the launch of the Hurling Development Committee in the *Irish Times* in September 2024 he wrote: 'This is a ground war. The challenge will be to identify places and people who want hurling to be part of their communities and shower them with support and resources . . . People must want it. They must have a feeling for it.'

Two previous national leaders in hurling, Paudie Butler and Martin Fogarty, saw their role as going into places where hurling was weak and meeting people, taking training sessions, and spreading the gospel in the most hands-on manner possible. When Fogarty left that role in 2021, he wasn't replaced for almost three years. If the name of the role has changed, we can reasonably expect the role itself to have changed as well. It will be Willie Maher's responsibility to find people who want to promote the game, and then support them with money and resources. And it will be his job to get county boards to ring-fence time: to set aside enough fixture weekends for hurling so that the game gets the oxygen it needs.

Hurling costs money – it is a far more expensive sport to play than football. The GAA has already committed to funding the expansion of hurling. The association had revenues of over €130 million in 2024, with a surplus of €6.3 million, even taking into account a 9 per cent decrease in government funding year on year. The GAA has already made a massive investment in coaching and games-development structures. They're in place, ready to be built on. The Táin Óg and CúChulainn leagues, which began in 2018, already provide a programme of games between clubs that have a shortage of opponents in their own counties. Four hundred games took place across the competitions at under-14, under-16, under-18, and adult levels in 2024.

I spoke to Declan Bogue, a GAA journalist from Lisbellaw in Fermanagh, about how they have created a hurling infrastructure in that county in the past ten years. Fermanagh were in the lowest of the five seven-team divisions in the national hurling league in 2025, but they won the Lory Meagher Cup in 2024, and they now have seven clubs playing juvenile hurling. Much of that growth is down to the Shane Mulholland Foundation. Shane was a Fermanagh hurler who passed away in 2015, after which his family created the foundation to promote youth hurling in Fermanagh and in surrounding counties. The money it raises has helped clubs start a hurling team, and keep it going. The game has a foothold in the county now in a way that it never has had before. It can be done.

In January 2023, Tooreen in Mayo and Easkey in Sligo went to Croke Park to play in the All-Ireland intermediate and junior club finals. If you look at the teams that usually play in those finals, it is the intermediate and junior champions of Kilkenny, Cork, Galway, Waterford, and Limerick. But the GAA allows the senior champions from weaker counties to compete against lower-level teams from elite counties, and they have been able to hold their own. I played in the Waterford Junior B championship, and I know the quality of player competing at that level. What Tooreen and Easkey achieved is no small feat.

Jarlath Burns had something else to say at Congress in 2025 about the expansion of hurling, beyond endorsing Liam Griffin's withdrawn motion. In the context of two seismic changes that have occurred in the GAA since 2020 (embracing a split season and redrawing the rules of Gaelic football), he said:

It is now hurling's time.

Yes, the Munster championship and the battle for the Liam MacCarthy Cup are the most awe-inspiring competitions you will find anywhere in world sport. But the duty we have to sustain them and the responsibility we shoulder for hurling beyond those competitions requires the sort of vision and bravery that have characterized our approach to grabbing the nettles that were the split season and football.

The actions we need to take need to be long term and sustainable, and we need to show leadership and resolve to do the right thing when it comes to growing the game, playing the game, and establishing new teams.

I'll make no apologies for living up to the mantle passed onto us by Michael Cusack that we preserve this great game, protect it and promote it so that every young boy and girl in Ireland has the chance to know the thrill of following in Setanta's footsteps.

I've already mentioned Paul Rouse's *The Hurlers*. In it he recounts the first ever Dublin hurling championship, in which Faugh-a-Ballaghs lost a classic game against Metropolitans in Elm Park in March 1887. Soon after, they lost again in the senior football championship, 'which they had been considered favourites to win'.

Rouse writes: 'The club secretary had no doubt it was their dual commitment that had cost them: "It is doubtful whether any club is able under these circumstances to carry off a championship, so expert have many clubs become who devote themselves to one or the other form of athletics."'

That's how long GAA clubs and counties have been wrestling with this issue. I sympathize with those who don't feel they can do it, but I still believe there's a duty on us all to try. Having lived it for a year, I can say it's 100 per cent worth it.

Cusack 'resolved to bring back the hurling'. And it's no accident that his name is invoked when people are determined to bring the game forward to pastures new. When you think of what he endeavoured to save – a game played in a few outposts, organized haphazardly, and with only the occasional curiosity of the outside world to sustain it – it sounds suspiciously like hurling in most of the northern half of the country over the past hundred years.

There are people, like our Scadán in Milltown, who rowed against the tide in their native place for years without ever managing to establish hurling. The GAA have shown in recent years that the way things used to be need not dictate how they will always be. If the will is there, then maybe this generation of Scadáns will be supported and encouraged to grow the game and realize Cusack's ambition in full, just in time for that dream's 150th birthday.

18

I stayed up in Dublin the night of the All-Ireland final, and went to see my physio/witch-doctor on Monday morning. Whatever magic she performed on my back appeared to work, and I was able to tog out for our last group game, against Geraldine's, the following weekend, which we won by a couple of points – though we made very hard work of it. In the end, only one sub was brought on, and obviously that wasn't me, but I felt afterwards that my back had made a full recovery.

For a newly promoted team to win four group games from four was a huge achievement. And yet the feeling around the team was that there was still a lot in us. That first half against Abbeyside in An Rinn had been really good, but otherwise we had only played in fits and starts.

We qualified straight to the West Waterford semi-finals, while there were a pair of quarter-finals involving the teams who finished second and third in the two groups of five. We had two weeks to prepare, and I was determined to keep improving my game.

Cormo's words were ringing in my ear: 'Don't be the worst at training.' This was my guiding principle. Some evenings I managed it – but it wasn't easy, because the team was buzzing. I found it hard to keep my feet on the ground, and thoughts of a West Waterford final were occupying uncomfortably large parts of my day.

This was fuelled in no small way by the possible presence in the opposing dressing room of Dan Shanahan, one of the most charismatic, beloved, and talented hurlers of this century.

If hurling loves its icons more than most sports, it loves its goal-scorers most of all, and Dan is one of the greats. He scored eight goals for Waterford on the way to winning the Player of the Year award in 2007, and he ended his inter-county career with four Munster championship medals. His club, Lismore, had topped the other group in our division and were hotly tipped to come through the other semi-final.

Two years before, Dan – already well into his forties – had played his thirtieth consecutive championship season with Lismore's first team, and the nation had saluted an amazing, possibly never-to-be-repeated feat. No one told Dan, though, because he went out and played senior championship in 2023 as well. And, making use of the provisions of a Waterford GAA by-law, he was able to play fifteen minutes at the end of a game they were winning comfortably in their senior championship in 2024 to make it thirty-two years in a row, without forfeiting his eligibility to line out for the Lismore juniors.

I was becoming a slave to this narrative. If we won our semi-final, then the worst-case scenario was that Dan the Man would end our run in a West Waterford final. This would be bitterly disappointing on a sporting level, but from the point of view of a man moving down to Waterford on spec to play hurling, having your season ended by the most devastating goal-scorer in the history of Waterford hurling, and possibly their greatest ever cult hero, would cushion the blow considerably. Or there was the alternative. We beat Dan'd, win the West Waterford, get to hoist a trophy, and then see what happened in the county final. If we were to win ourselves a county final, and promotion to Junior A, then we'd be in dreamland. Happy days either way . . . as long as we won our semi-final.

A week out from that semi-final we discovered that we'd be playing Abbeyside again. We dealt with them fairly comfortably in the group stage, but the concern with a town club (Abbeyside is based in Dungarvan) was that they'd be able to pull young lads from out of nowhere to bolster their second team – guys who couldn't be bothered training for their senior team or who were just out of minor.

The game was fixed for Sunday at midday, in the Fraher Field in Dungarvan. On Thursday night, at training in Old Parish, that age-old fear hit again, the oldest feeling in the

GAA book: that this could be our last session of the year. In the church of the GAA, you do not know the day or the hour. Some years you see it coming, and some years you don't.

The Thursday before the semi-final was one of those evenings at training when I felt like I had something to build on – a couple of nice finishes when through on goal, an infuriating habit of following a good piece of play with a terrible one. But it was fun. So much fun.

Sunday would be another step on the way . . . unless, of course, it wasn't.

The weather that Sunday morning was absolutely horrendous. It was the middle of August, but it felt like a morning in February, a cold fog rolling in off the estuary in Dungarvan. The rain was coming down pretty heavily – so heavily that it lessened not just your chances of catching the ball, but of holding your hurley firmly in your hand.

We were warming up on the end of Fraher Field furthest from the sea. I was reminding myself that I needed to focus extra hard on my first touch, and on my handling, in conditions like this, when Tadhg came over to me and told me to focus on precisely those two things 'when you come on'. This sharpened the focus still further. I was not taking Tadhg's remark as a guarantee of anything, but it was at least an indication that if things were going well, they were eager to get me in.

The weather ruined the game as a spectacle, but we led 6 points to 5 at half-time, and then stretched our lead out to 11–5 with little more than ten minutes to go. In a game with so few scores, it looked like a bigger lead than six points usually is in hurling.

And then utter calamity struck. First, Abbeyside went for goal from a 25-metre free, on the angle. It flew into our net for their first score of the second half. They got a second goal three minutes later, from a mix-up in our defence, and out of nowhere our lead was gone. Then we conceded a free from our own puck-out, and suddenly we were down. We missed a couple of chances, and in the first minute of injury time, Abbeyside got a third goal. We got a goal either side of two points by them but it wasn't enough. We were out, beaten 3–8 to 1–11.

We had played four games without conceding a goal in the group stages, a fair achievement at any level of hurling. We'd gone another fifty minutes of hurling without conceding one here . . . only to then give away three in ten minutes and lose the game. It was devastating.

I've sat in a lot of losing dressing rooms, and this one was as bad as any I'd ever been in. I hadn't gotten on in the end, given how tight the game had been, but that hardly mattered. It felt utterly horrendous. Some championship defeats can feel like you've been fighting to get out of quicksand for hours before it enveloped you. You kicked, you screamed, but in the end gravity had its way. You at least had time to get used to the idea that the end was nigh, even as you were fighting to avoid it.

This was more like falling down a manhole as you were serenely making your way down the street.

I threw my helmet in the boot of the car and reckoned all of a sudden with the idea that my hurling experience was over. We headed to the pub, we talked, we gave out, and we dealt with it. But we had lost. No amount of talking was going to change that.

And Dan the Man had won his semi-final. This one was going to hurt for a while.

I return again to that line from the George Plimpton documentary: did I capture my 'perfect moment of total failure'? Was that even what I was looking for? I suppose I had wanted to play the game and understand it better, as a sporting endeavour and as a cultural monolith in our country, and in the five months since I'd started training with An Sean Phobal I'd discovered plenty.

There's a reason that Loughnane line resonates, the one about starting at seven years old before it's too late. To become an instinctive hurler is hard, because the basic skills of the game are so difficult to master. To get to a level of basic proficiency takes a phenomenal amount of work – you're giving yourself a much better chance of success if you start in school, and not in your forties.

Hurling, like swimming or a foreign language, gets

progressively more difficult with every year you don't learn it in childhood. Taught at six or seven, it has a chance to become a thing that you'll never forget, like riding a bike.

I have a hard time accepting that hurling is conclusively a skill you gain either in childhood or not at all – but of course starting early makes things far simpler. There was a small part of me that thought that I might actually be able to conquer it, with the help of organized training sessions, games, ball-walls. That same part of me felt, after my first training session, that I had it cracked if I could catch and pass the odd ball. Such confidence, of course, proved misplaced. It was frustrating to learn the hard way how wrong I had been, but also oddly reassuring. *This thing that you heard was hard? Yeah, it's really fucking hard.* And the process of banging my head up against the difficulty of hurling was so enriching.

There are a number of questions that I've been asked since the season ended, primarily by football lovers anxious to be told the truth, unvarnished and hard to hear as it may be: Is hurling more enjoyable to play than football?

I can, of course, speak only for myself. One answer is that I enjoyed the games of Gaelic football I played in 2024 more than I did the hurling, for the simple reason that I could contribute something useful. I felt pressure and responsibility, but not to any oppressive degree; and I naturally enjoyed having a sense of basic mastery of the core skills and a sense that I could affect the game positively. By contrast, the best I could hope for in hurling games was that I be ignorable.

It's also true that the hurling games I took part in were filled with examples of outstanding skill, moments that were testament to years of practice and immersion in the game. Much of the pleasure I derived from playing in those matches or watching from the sideline was linked to a sense of proximity to those skills and that immersion.

Patrick Conway hit a point in our first championship game that was pure self-expression. The ball was passed to him, and he controlled it on his hurley – never taking it into his hand – before arrowing it over the bar. It was just a joy to watch.

I could also talk about the neatness and precision of Diarmuid Ó Curraoin's touch and passing. Declan Ryan's defensive nous, and the sharpness of touch that was an indication of the years of senior hurling he'd played with Midleton in Cork before he moved to Old Parish. Conor French's and Andrew Hourigan's work rate and physicality, Simon Lawrence's ability in the air.

And this is Junior B hurling in Waterford! The dedication required to move up through the grades and continue to improve one's touch and handling, to get yourself into a physical condition to be able to express yourself, is mind-boggling. And yet that's the goal that An Sean Phobal's players set for themselves. The club has a cohort of young players who make up the spine of the team, and they have a terrific opportunity to keep progressing.

Football people have also asked me a related but very different question: Is hurling just *better* than football?

Hurling as it's being played now allows more space for the spontaneous, for the beautiful, than football — yes, even at Junior B. It is better to watch, and more enjoyable to play for the most skilful players. Old Parish have some exceptional forwards, and they got plenty of close attention from opposition teams, but they were still able to have an impact on the game. In hurling, these players are not stifled in the way the best footballers often are. Hurling is too open a game to allow it.

While hurling requires skills that are harder to attain and more breathtaking to watch than the skills of Gaelic football, it is also in many ways a simpler game. We went out and hurled fifteen on fifteen, without sweepers or zonal marking. None of our opponents offered us any other tactical picture than that. All my previous experience of Gaelic football, by contrast, would have seen a bit of defensive, safety-first stuff, no matter how low the level. As you go up the ranks in both codes, there is obviously more tactical variation; but it seems to me the difference between hurling and football remains the same all the way along.

Hurlers were happier to attend to their own job and mind their own corner than Gaelic footballers, too. We had a few tireless runners who were able to join attacks from the half-back line in hurling, but for the most part, unless you were switched from one position to another, you stayed in your zone and you tried to win your personal battle. There were far fewer of the never-ending support runs required of you in Gaelic football, and lots more lengthy clearances to allow defenders a chance to take a breather. No one in the An Sean Phobal dressing room was complaining about any of this.

There's a joy in the fulfilment of even the easiest tasks on a hurling field. A ball comes towards you. You control it, it comes into your hand, you advance ten metres with the ball on your stick, you pick out a pass to a teammate thirty metres away. Neat, tidy hurling. Your touch, your vision and your stick-passing are all tested, and all showcased. What's not to like about that?

In Gaelic football, that level of pressure on the basic skills just isn't there. Most of the time you're knitting together passages of possession, trying to take on players only when you have options to your left and right. In fact, trying anything in football which is as hard as even the most nondescript of hurling functions is generally considered too risky.

Possession is ten-tenths of the law to Gaelic football coaches, particularly when facing a massed defence. If you hold the ball and do literally nothing with it for four minutes, then you're controlling the clock and denying the opposition a chance to do something. The most frustrating thing from a spectator's point of view is that defending teams are often happier to let that happen than to try and win the ball back. That mode of thinking on both the offensive and defensive side of things, which is now completely endemic in the game, doesn't challenge anyone's skills. Any half-decent club player could hand-pass the ball backwards every time they got it, if they'd the fitness to keep running up and down the field tracking runners when they're out of possession.

In hurling, gaining possession is hard enough even when you're standing on your own. And holding on to it meaninglessly is not an option, because there's no such thing as a blanket defence in hurling – it would be impossible to adequately cover a scoring zone that stretches a hundred metres from your own goal, so it's pointless even trying.

There are sweepers at the highest level of hurling, but their intent is to squeeze the space in front of an opponent's full-forward line, not to preclude them from scoring out the field. Hurling is still full of turnovers – it's too difficult to hold on to the ball for that not to be the case. And that makes it a supremely enjoyable sport both to watch and to play.

If training in An Sean Phobal started at 7.30 p.m., the management would be down at the pitch at 7 o'clock with a bag of sliotars, in case guys wanted to work on their striking – frees, sideline cuts, and puck-outs. Whenever possible I was down there at 7 o'clock as well, just noodling about for the most part but also trying to get used to the idea of taking shots at goal while moving, or at least in vaguely game-specific situations like getting a hand-pass from a colleague with his back to goal, waiting for you to strike it over the bar.

Those non-pressure situations were also great times to work on attacking the ball, not waiting for it to come to you. Each skill you learned was just a stepping-stone to the next level. So if, by the end of June, I was reasonably confident that I could kill and control a pass coming at me from twenty metres, now I had to try to make sure that I was tearing out towards that ball, not anxiously waiting for it to come onto my hurl.

That part of it was a lot of fun as well.

Dad was down in Waterford a few times over the summer, and he was at training one evening (because it was impossible to keep him away, quite frankly). He was behind the goal as I emerged from a ruck of bodies and, with a flick of my wrist, managed to get the ball off the ground, away from the ruck, and into my hand. I took on the player in front of me, made room for a shot . . . and arrowed it just over rather than just under the bar.

The speed of the pick-up, the effectiveness of the carry, and the near-perfection of the finish came pretty much from nowhere, and even now, months after I did it, the almost ridiculous memory of it pops into my mind completely unbidden. I was so annoyed I hadn't stuck it in the top corner, just for Dad . . . but he said I was moving pretty well, and if he wanted to leave with an extremely misleading portrait of the state of my game that evening, then I wasn't going to contradict him.

There was another moment, at training five days before our semi-final defeat, when I was given a pass about thirty metres from goal, on the right-hand side of our attack. I caught it first time, and felt my marker on my back, too close to me. If I got turned I knew I could use his proximity against him – and I did. As he barrelled into me, I stepped across him, his momentum was broken, and I was away. He tried to pull across me, but I carried the ball ten metres in towards goal and then found the shot I'd been looking for when Dad had been there a few weeks before. It crashed off the underside of the crossbar and in, and I could hear Sean and Tadhg roaring their approval. In that moment, I felt like a hurler. I can't think of that moment – as I often do – without also acknowledging that instead of sticking my chest out and dominating the rest of the session, I dropped the next four balls that came in to me. Normal rules about feeling confident or not feeling confident just didn't apply. I simply hadn't done the reps to be able to feel like I'd just always improve. If it felt like a miracle when the odd good thing happened, maybe that's because it was.

19

I went golfing with Michael Hogan the Tuesday after our defeat. Instead of a West Waterford final to look forward to, all we had was a post-mortem.

Michael was one of the best footballers to have ever played for An Sean Phobal, and he had played inter-county for years. He had also been involved at county board level for a long time, and so he had experienced the GAA from just about every conceivable angle. He had never played hurling in his life – there was no hurling in the club in his day – but he was club chairman, and he wasn't any better at losing to three goals in the last ten minutes than I was.

We were supposed to change tack now and focus on the football championship, which would start in three weeks' time, in mid-September. This was the way it was done in Waterford. We were all too sick to train that week, and every day we weren't back in action with the big ball we were losing whatever benefit we'd gotten from going out of the hurling a couple of weeks early.

In the previous three years, An Sean Phobal's hurling season had gone all the way to county final weekend – which left only a week for the transition from hurling to football. If you were ambitious about your hurling and had a squad with a number of players based away from home, then you were training exclusively as a hurling team any time you got a chance to train.

Now that we were out, it felt like it would have been a good idea if we had kept the football ticking over throughout the summer; but as the summer unfolded there was never a moment when I felt we should be spending any of our training time looking ahead to a football game in September. That might have had a lot to do with my own selfish obsession with trying to get better at hurling, but I don't think I was out of step with too many of my teammates.

This year, with a bit more time to switch into football mode, there was some small hope that we'd be able to capitalize.

My priorities had changed somewhat during the summer. I had come down for a few months to try to play hurling, and I wanted to play football to deepen my connection to the club, and maybe to try to drive things if I could, having been of little or no use with the small ball. That remained the plan . . . but something else had happened. I'd fallen heavily in love with the place. And so had Gill, who had spent the summer trying to concoct ways to move down here permanently.

We had gotten very close to my cousins in An Rinn, Gill had swimming companions she couldn't bear to say goodbye to, and we were almost dreading a return to city life. Towards the end of August my cousin Bríd had told me that she'd heard from two different people that 'that cousin of hers in Old Parish' was moving down permanently. I told her to confirm any such rumours immediately, and to burnish them as ridiculously as she saw fit in future. It wasn't anything my wife and I weren't discussing anyway.

Gill and I spoke often about her chances of getting a job down here (pretty good), the problems posed by my working from down here (nigh-on insuperable), and then the various compromises and accommodations that would be required to make it work in some form or another.

We did it idly to begin with, but as the summer went on the conversations became more animated, the resolutions more concrete. We had spent six weeks living in the cottage in Kilgobinet, in a house big enough to have friends and family down to visit, and then we'd spent two months in An Sean Phobal, in a smaller place just for ourselves. But it wasn't enough. We found another place in Old Parish to live Thursday to Sunday for September and October, while we worked in Dublin. We weren't ready to say goodbye just yet. I could make it down to Old Parish in time for football training after work on Thursdays, Gill would follow me down on Fridays after school. Following an inauspicious beginning, training had grown more animated and better attended as we got closer to our opening group game. I came to believe that the season depended on the result of that first game in mid-September.

I felt in my heart that the young lads who were the driving force of the club were hurlers first – the Flynns, the Ó Mathúna brothers, Conor French, Andrew Hourigan, Luke Wade. They were still devastated by how the hurling had finished, and we absolutely had to win our first game to flush that out of our system.

And we had chances to beat Tallow that first day out. To be more precise, I had chances. I was handed two clear-cut goal opportunities, but one was saved and the other one skimmed the crossbar and went over rather than under. If both of those had gone in, I'm convinced we'd have won. But we lost, and now that we were under a bit of pressure in the group, I feared the worst.

We played Lismore the next day out, and lost a game we should have won by eight or nine points to a last-minute goal (with Dan the Man making an appearance off the bench, it should be said. So I played on the same pitch as him – but it was the big ball, so it didn't really hit the same way).

It was always likely that a few lads on every team in the competition (and they were nearly all dual clubs) would struggle to refocus so soon after the hurling championship, and that's how it proved. It certainly affected me: not having played football for three months, my own sharpness was way off where it needed to be to start with. We definitely should have won those first two group games, but maybe we got out of them what we put into them. That was really hard to take.

Finishing bottom of our football group meant we'd have to win a relegation play-off to ensure we stayed in Junior A for 2025. We played Stradbally on the first really cold night of the year, a Friday evening in mid-October in Dungarvan, and we conceded another last-minute goal and drew the thing. We'd have to go again a week later.

On the Sunday afternoon of that same weekend, my nephew Enda was playing for Athenry in the Galway Minor A hurling final against Oranmore-Maree. It was a bitterly cold afternoon, and I got the train down from Dublin that morning. I walked from the station a full hour before the game was due to start, and of course my mother and father were parked outside the ground before I'd even gotten off the train.

Dad was nervous – he had woken up at 5 a.m. and couldn't get back to sleep. He'd been nervous all week. Mam was telling me she was fine, but I could tell she was a little on edge too.

We walked into the ground together, and my brother Paul, Enda's dad, was just inside the gate. My cousin Sean, his wife Aoife, and their three kids landed in soon after.

Another brother, John, was in a couple of minutes later. Along with Enda's two younger brothers and his mother Nicola, there were twelve of us sitting in a row in the stand waiting for the game to start. Enda was in midfield, as he had been in every county final he'd played with his age group. And at under-13, under-14, under-15, and under-16 they had finished the year as the best team in the county. But the minor (under-17) title was the one that everyone wanted. This would be his last game with the lads who had been his mates from the very start of his hurling career. As the throw-in neared, I felt so nervous for him.

Athenry aren't my club, obviously, but we'd watched this group for the past six or seven years, so Mam and Dad in particular knew all the kids on the team. I was trying not to shout purely for Enda, but I knew how much it mattered to him. He had been overlooked for the Galway minor team earlier in the year, and this is naturally a devastating thing to happen to a kid, particularly given that he had been selected at midfield for the first game at the county under-15 grade two summers earlier.

When he got the news about the Galway minors in February, it knocked him back. But as the year progressed, the Athenry under-20 team came looking for him, and he ended up playing at midfield for them before his seventeenth birthday, which gave him a big boost in confidence at a vital moment. It showed him that all the things he offered a hurling team were very much respected by his own. And from the start of the minor county final he played like a man possessed. Watching it from the new perspective that my own time playing the game had given me, I was so impressed by his selflessness, his desire to be a good teammate, his skill, his heart.

The game was level at half-time, and then Oranmore-Maree got two goals in the first minute of the second half. With his team in a massive hole, Enda thundered into the game all the harder. Athenry's best forward, Frank Burke, ended up scoring 1–13 in a county final, and so no one else was winning Man of the Match, but Enda was next in line.

Athenry had to withstand a 21-metre free, and then another goalmouth scramble, before they held on for a two-point win. The crowd in Kenny Park was huge for an under-17 game, over a thousand people, and the roar at the end was deafening. I tried to pick out Paul on the opposite terrace (he was too nervous to watch it with the rest of us), and then I saw him down on the field as Enda charged at him, knocking him to the ground in his enthusiasm.

I remember distinctly when Enda was seven or eight, and Paul told me in our parents' house in Milltown that he himself had started to learn the correct technique to strike the ball, lift the ball, hand-pass the ball ... because if Enda wanted to be good, he'd have to practise at home, and Paul wanted that practice to be perfect. So he learned the correct grip for himself – two hands on the hurley, put up your hand – and tried to pass those principles on to Enda. Paul understood something that might not even register with people in traditionally strong hurling counties. The level of inter-generational training that is passed on in the home from parent to child is what will keep those counties ahead of the rest for the foreseeable future. Hurling is not a sport you can spend an hour a week training for – you need to work on it at home. If your parents hurled, then that learning is passed on throughout the week. Watching Paul take that on was my first up-close, inside-the-family experience of the dedication required to gain competence at hurling. You could very easily draw a line from that moment to my summer, in fact: Enda's hurling career was one of the things I hoped to understand better by spending a summer hurling myself.

The standard of Galway underage hurling is ridiculous. As well as all those county titles, Enda's team had also won the Galway Féile competition, and they were the only Galway team in the last six years that hadn't gone on to win the All-Ireland Féile final. If you're the best underage team in Galway, you've an excellent chance of being the best team in your age-grade in the country. The clubs are obviously doing exceptional work, and the quality of the basics from every single player, subs and all, on both teams in this county final was amazingly high.

At one stage in the first half, with Athenry under the cosh, their corner-back was bottled up in the right corner of their defence. Enda stood twenty metres out from his own goal, demanded the ball off his corner-back, took the pass, and then sprayed the ball out to his wing-forward sixty metres downfield.

Leadership, to drop back in and help his defence. Trust, to call for the pass, and to be given it by his corner-back. Calmness and composure, to pick out the pass from underneath his own goalposts effectively. And skill, to execute the pass under pressure. The whole package.

An Sean Phobal's footballers had our relegation play-off replay the week after Enda's final, in a gale in Colligan, and we managed to secure our survival in Junior A football. It wasn't the win to finish off the season that I had hoped for (I had dreamed of a county final), but nevertheless it was a novel experience for me to finish a championship campaign with a victory. In fact, it had never happened to me before. I had played well, finally, and it was a relief to have been able to contribute something.

I went back to my uncle John's house for dinner, with his wife Marian and her brother Paul. This was the house my grandmother had lived in for all my life. When I was a kid we would only see her twice or three times a year, when my dad would bring us all to his home place for a week in summertime, or when she would get the bus up to us in Galway for a few days. I remember Dad taking her for long spins with us, out the roads to Lismore or Cappoquin or onto Youghal. She was a beautiful soul, a person who lived for fun and laughter and family. I wrote her letters, and she used to spoil me rotten. When she died in 2004, I felt as though my link to Waterford had changed and weakened irreparably. I had never reckoned with that feeling until now, after it had been comprehensively disproven.

I still hadn't found a picture of her husband Patsy, my grandfather who'd died eight years before I was born, which I'd promised to show Mick Dunford, the man in Kilgobinet who had known him when he was young. I was ashamed to say that I didn't have a clear image in my head of what Patsy looked like. I knew that he was a small man, and that Dad's height, and I suppose our height as boys, came from my grandmother's side. But suddenly there he was, an image from ninety years ago or more, scanned onto a computer and forwarded to me by my brother.

Patsy was dressed up in a three-piece suit that might have seen better days, with a pen and a pocket square in his breast pocket. His hair was coiffed in a style that would be familiar to customers of a Brooklyn coffee shop – swept back in a mountainous quiff, cut short on the sides. A large, Roman nose, exactly like mine and like his son John's. He couldn't have denied John, anyway, and yet he looked exactly like me too. And for the first time

I saw myself in my uncle as well. Maybe this whole idea, the whole summer of hurling, was the sort of daft caper only John would try to pull off. But I had gone and done it regardless.

After dinner, John had some farming to do just outside Dungarvan – he had cows in a field, next to a house he and Marian had just inherited from her uncle. John had some painters in there that week, and so he let me into the house to see the work in progress. 'It's as dry as a bone, even though it hasn't been lived in for a couple of years.'

It really was a beautiful little place.

'You know, if you wanted to stay here next summer we'd be delighted to have you. You'd just have to feed those calves out in the field beside you there.'

I looked around. He might have been joking about the calves, but of course I could count them every morning, make sure none of them had gotten into trouble. And then if I spotted a gap in the fence, I'd learn how to mend that . . . wouldn't be any issue there, I'm sure it's an easy enough job. In fact, I'm pretty sure Gill would enjoy it even more than I would. That back room would be a nice writing room . . . or maybe the little conservatory in front, that would be lovely too. I would catch the morning sun there. The dog would love the front yard. Might not love the calves, of course, but she'd get used to them, or vice versa. Tempting to dream, isn't it?

John: 'Of course, there'd be no talk of retirement now. You'd have to play football next year too, that's just the cost of doing business with a man such as myself.'

I considered this for a moment. 'And you'd need me to tog out for the hurlers too, surely – you'd hate to see them denied my talents?'

John's eyes, dancing. A smile as wide as Dungarvan Bay.

Acknowledgements

I'd like to thank sincerely all the people of Old Parish. You gave us the summer of our lives – and as your reward, you'll never be able to get rid of us.

Ba mhaith liom buíochas a ghlacadh freisin le mo chomhimreoirí go léir; Tadhg Murphy; agus go háirithe Sean Wade. Bhí sé an-speisialta an geansaí dearg agus bán a chaitheamh. Up the Shocks.

It was such a pleasure to be able to spend a year with my darling aunt Joan, and with my cousins in An Rinn. Thank you to the Mounfoun wing of the family – with Marian, Sinéad, and the great John Murphy . . . we had some fun, didn't we? Thank you to the indomitable Deaglán Ó Murchú and Beatrice in Waterford city too.

Michael and Ann Hogan and their family have been so helpful and kind to Gill and me, all summer and since. We treasure you all.

Sincere thanks to Jamie Wall and Paul Rouse for their unstinting support and advice – so much of this work relied on your wise counsel and experience. And a special word too for Sinéad O'Carroll, whose camogie retirement I'm still refusing to accept. Thank you to everyone who gave their time to talk to me and help me fill in the gaps in my Hurling Man CV . . . too many to mention here but particular thanks to Declan Lawn, Neil McManus, Michael Duignan, and Liam Griffin. And the great Jim Carney, of course!

Brendan Barrington is an incredibly gifted, patient, brilliant editor and I feel so lucky to have been able to work with him again. Heartfelt thanks to Michael McLoughlin and all at Penguin Sandycove, and to Conor Nagle.

To my Second Captains family — I had to rely on your good graces to make this happen, and you were all so supportive and understanding. You're special people.

To Mark Horgan, and to all my other friends who have spent the past couple of years navigating life and all its vicissitudes. You've given me support and inspiration at every turn.

Thank you to my parents, and to my brothers.

And a final thank you to Gill — who, to everyone's surprise but her own, discovered her best life in west Waterford.